SpringerBriefs in Environment, Security, Development and Peace

Volume 41

Series Editor

Hans Günter Brauch, Peace Research and European Security Studies, Mosbach, Germany

This peer-reviewed book series addresses topics in four major research programmes in the social and political sciences and in international relations: a) environmental studies or ecology; b) international, national and human security studies; c) development studies; and d) peace studies or peace research; and the six dyadic conceptual relationships between them: (i) peace and security; (ii) peace and environment; (iii) development and security; (iv) environment and development (sustainable development); (v) development and security; and (vi) environment and security.

These four key concepts and the six dyadic conceptual relationships address significant issues in international politics and in international relations but also in many other disciplines in the social and natural sciences. The SpringerBriefs in Environment, Security, Development and Peace (ESDP) address the linkages across disciplines, and the editor welcomes book proposals and completed manuscripts by natural and social scientists, as well as by multidisciplinary teams of authors. The material may address issues of global change and its impacts on humankind, on environmentally-induced migration, on crises and conflicts, as well as proposing cooperative strategies to cope with these challenges either locally or in the framework of international organizations and regimes. These SpringerBriefs present concise summaries of cutting-edge research and innovative policy perspectives. The series focuses on the interconnection of the new and non-traditional global environmental and development challenges that face humankind and that may pose dangers to peace and security in the Anthropocene era of earth history. SpringerBriefs in ESDP publish short monographs and edited volumes of workshops that are peer-reviewed by scholars from many disciplines and from all parts of the world. These SpringerBriefs will give more voice and visibility to scientists and innovative political thinkers in developing countries. SpringerBriefs in ESDP provide multi-, inter- and transdisciplinary knowledge relevant for coping with the numerous projected impacts of global environmental change, political, economic and cultural crises and conflicts. They offer

- Timely state-of-the art analyses (e.g. of earth systems science, geoecology) and policy assessments of the global challenges facing humankind in the 21st century
- Bridges between new research results with snapshots of hot and/or emerging topics, literature reviews and in-depth case studies.

Imtiaz Ahmed · ASM Ali Ashraf ·
Niloy Ranjan Biswas

Handbook on Deradicalization and Rehabilitation of Violent Extremist Offenders in Bangladesh

Springer

Imtiaz Ahmed
Centre for Alternatives
Dhaka, Bangladesh

ASM Ali Ashraf
Department of International Relations
University of Dhaka
Dhaka, Bangladesh

Niloy Ranjan Biswas
Department of International Relations
University of Dhaka
Dhaka, Bangladesh

ISSN 2193-3162 ISSN 2193-3170 (electronic)
SpringerBriefs in Environment, Security, Development and Peace
ISBN 978-3-031-85806-2 ISBN 978-3-031-85807-9 (eBook)
https://doi.org/10.1007/978-3-031-85807-9

This Springer imprint is published by the registered company Springer Nature Switzerland AG
The registered company address is: Gewerbestrasse 11, 6330 Cham, Switzerland

Acknowledgements

The *Handbook on Deradicalization and Rehabilitation of Violent Extremist Offenders in Bangladesh* is the outcome of a collaborative research initiative that spanned 8 months (August 2022–March 2023). It builds on an earlier phase (November 2021–March 2022) of collaborative research titled *Rehabilitation and Reintegration of Violent Extremist Offenders in Bangladesh.*

The research team acknowledges continuous support from the Sasakawa Peace Foundation for this study. We thank Dr. Muhammad Kamruzzaman Mozumder, Professor of Clinical Psychology, University of Dhaka; Ms. Mahfuza Liza, BPM, Special Superintendent of Police (Internal Affairs), Special Branch, Bangladesh Police; Mr. Nur Mohammad Ali Chisty, Additional Superintendent of Police, Anti-terrorism Unit, Bangladesh Police; and Mr. Md Nazmul Islam, Assistant Commissioner of Police, Counter Terrorism and Transnational Crime, Dhaka Metropolitan Police, Bangladesh Police, for their valuable inputs in this study. We also thank the Research Associates, Mr. Saidul Islam, Ms. Marzia Al-Hakeem, Ms. Tasnim Rahman Nira, Mr. Md Humaun Kabir, and Mr. F. M. Arafat, for meticulously helping us with the research.

Among those mentioned here, Dr. Kamruzzaman Mozumder and Mr. Saidul Islam made substantive contributions to the chapter on psychological intervention, Mr. Chisty in the chapter on resettlement support, and Ms. Liza and Mr. Nazmul Islam to the chapter on legal counseling. Finally, thanks also to the Research Assistants, Mr. Mahi Nur-e-Aziz, Mr. Khandaker Tahmid Rezwan, and Mr. Nur Nahar Shukanna, for helping us with the logistics, particularly when convening an endless number of meetings.

The research team is grateful to various individuals and stakeholders for their crucial assistance in data collection. Senior officials from Bangladesh Police and its different constituting bodies, including the Anti-terrorism Unit, the Counter Terrorism and Transnational Crime (CTTC) Unit of Dhaka Metropolitan Police, and the Rapid Action Battalion, deserve special thanks for sharing valuable archival documents and facilitating our field works.

We sincerely appreciate the Directorate General of Forces Intelligence, the National Security Intelligence, and the Special Branch for providing privileged access to high-profile interviews. Special thanks to the Prisons Directorate for their support in understanding existing prison management and the scope for introducing prisons-based deradicalization and rehabilitation programs.

We are indebted to several individuals and institutions for facilitating our field trips to Indonesia and Singapore in December 2022. Among them, Bangladesh High Commissioner to Indonesia, Air Vice Marshal Mohammad Mustafizur Rahman, GUP, ndc, PSC, and Bangladesh High Commissioner to Singapore, Md Tauhedul Islam, ndc, and senior embassy officials in both countries deserve special thanks for connecting us to essential stakeholders. In Indonesia, senior officials from the National Counter Terrorism Agency BNPT, the Directorate General of Corrections, the Ministry of Interior, the Ministry of Justice, and the Coordinating Ministry for Political, Legal, and Security Affairs shared their national best practices. In Singapore, senior officials from the Ministry of Home Affairs offered valuable insights into their current trends in violent extremism, deradicalization, and rehabilitation.

We were privileged to hear from academic scholars and civil society organizations about their views on the challenges of deradicalization and rehabilitation in Southeast Asia. Special thanks are due to senior researchers at the Universitas Indonesia, Universitas Muhammadiyah, Nanyang Technology University, and the National University of Singapore. The Habibie Center, the Society against Radicalism and Violent Extremism (SeRVE), and independent deradicalization experts in Indonesia and Singapore were always accessible when we needed their views.

We thank 30 Bangladeshi interviewees with various legal statuses (convicts, under-trial detainees, surrendered militants, and former ethno-nationalist rebels) for sharing their belief systems and candid views. We also thank interviews from various experts in Bangladesh who represent the government, private sector, and civil society. While many people have directly or indirectly contributed to the drafting of this Handbook and the research behind it, the research team is solely responsible for any acts of commission or omission.

Executive Summary

This *Handbook on Deradicalization and Rehabilitation of Violent Extremist Offenders in Bangladesh* is developed in the context of rising threats of terrorism posed by a wide variety of violent extremist (VE) groups. It has 18 chapters. The abstracts for each chapter are presented below:

Chapter 1 (Introduction): This chapter has several sections. First, it offers a context analysis and justifies the rationale for adopting a Handbook like this. Next, it identifies several core principles such as gender sensitivity, respect for human rights and the rule of law, safety and security of target beneficiaries, inter-agency coordination, high-quality intelligence, and monitoring and evaluation. After defining some key terms, it then describes the target audience, which includes various stakeholders, including policymakers and legislators, counterterrorism practitioners and prison authorities, and other actors such as families, communities, and educational institutions. It also lists psychological and religious counselors in the target audience due to their essential roles in deradicalization and rehabilitation.

The Handbook adopts a whole-of-society approach and offers a four-pronged intervention plan to be implemented in four distinct stages:

- Preparatory stage;
- Deradicalization;
- Rehabilitation; and
- Policy issues.

Chapter 2 (Target Beneficiaries): This chapter provides a comprehensive list of six beneficiary groups: (a) convicted and imprisoned; (b) convicted but released after prison term; (c) under-trial detainees; (d) under-trial on bail; (e) surrendered but not imprisoned; and (f) at-risk communities. It also calls for addressing the deradicalization and rehabilitation needs of all categories of VEOs operating in Bangladesh. They represent three major ideological camps: ethno-nationalist, left-wing, and faith-based Islamist groups.

Chapter 3 (Key Actors): This chapter lists 14 key actors. It argues that law enforcement, intelligence agencies, and prison authorities are key implementing agencies. It emphasizes the role of psychologists, religious counselors, educational institutions, vocational and skills trainers, and cultural organizations for cognitive and ideological transformation and physical disengagement. Various rehabilitative activities call for the involvement of social workers, business chambers, families of VEOs and victims, civil society, and community gatekeepers. Finally, it suggests the involvement of political actors and the media.

Chapter 4 (Capacity Building of Prison Staff and CT Professionals): This chapter provides a plan for building the capacity of prison staff and CT professionals to implement and coordinate various activities designed for the deradicalization and rehabilitation of VEOs.

Chapter 5 (Screening and Admission for Assessing Readiness): This chapter presents the Militant Activity Risks and Needs Assessment (MARNA) as a basis for determining the readiness of target beneficiaries for deradicalization and rehabilitation. The MARNA tool has four components: risk assessment indicators, assessment scores, qualitative assessment, overall assessment, and intervention plan. It calls for a multi-stakeholder intervention involving security and intelligence agencies, forensic psychologists, and religious counselors.

Chapter 6 (Religious Counselling): As Islamist militancy has emerged as a significant security threat, this chapter calls for the engagement of religious scholars as a path toward the physical disengagement of VEOs. Among the various activities, it calls for developing a religious counseling module, a religious rehabilitation group, a mobile application, and modernizing Imam training.

Chapter 7 (Psychological Intervention): This chapter provides a list of activities to be carried out to disengage an individual from extremist ideas for cognitive behavioral transformation.

Chapter 8 (Cultural Orientation): This chapter highlights the role of cultural and sporting activities in creating a healthy society. Cultural orientation will be given by promoting Bangladeshi culture, heritage, and language and engaging the youth in various sporting competitions.

Chapter 9 (Social Harmony, Pluralism, and Tolerance Through Education): Tolerance education can play a crucial role in countering intolerance and violent extremism by promoting social harmony, pluralism, and tolerance. By providing the VEOs with a comprehensive and nuanced understanding of different cultures, religions, and perspectives, education can help them develop empathy and respect for others.

Chapter 10 (Legal Counselling): This chapter lays out a plan for CT professionals and legal aid service providers in Bangladesh to disseminate the knowledge of the Anti-terrorism Act and other relevant laws and policies as an instrument for C/PVE. It is assumed that knowledge of the emerging body of laws will prevent an individual from holding extremist ideas or planning to conduct a terrorist attack.

Chapter 11 (Physical Disengagement): This chapter discusses how an individual, whether a convict in prison, an under-trial suspect on bail, or a person vulnerable to recruitment and radicalization, can be physically disengaged from a terrorist activity or group. The roles of the prison authorities, CT agencies, families, and other social actors are emphasized in motivating, training, and monitoring an individual.

Chapter 12 (Academic Training): This chapter stresses the need to extend educational opportunities for various beneficiaries, such as those who could not finish their studies or wish to continue after an interval. It argues that education and skills will enhance critical thinking ability and enable a person to pursue a meaningful livelihood opportunity.

Chapter 13 (Vocational Skills Training): This chapter provides a plan for promoting technical and vocational education and training (TVET) as an instrument for deradicalization and rehabilitation.

Chapter 14 (Employment and Entrepreneurial Support): This chapter discusses the need for extending employment opportunities and entrepreneurial support to rehabilitate VEOs. The roles of CT agencies, business chambers, financial institutions, and prison authorities are highlighted. A need assessment tool is annexed to match the demand and supply sides.

Chapter 15 (Support for the Family and Community Members): VEOs' families and community members will be essential in implementing a deradicalization and rehabilitation strategy. Hence, this chapter discusses how CT agencies, counselors, and educational institutions can provide various support services to VEOs' families and communities.

Chapter 16 (Resettlement Support): This chapter proposes a multi-stakeholder plan for resettling a post-release convicted VEO. Physical resettlement, social reintegration, and surveillance are expected to be vital in implementing this plan.

Chapter 17 (Policy Reforms): This chapter stresses the need for a designed legal and policy framework for the deradicalization and rehabilitation of VEOs. The Ministry of Home Affairs (MoHA), in collaboration with other ministries of the Government of Bangladesh, will initiate the reforms. Some reforms are underway, such as the Bangladesh Police adopting the *CTTC Strategy for Countering Violent Extremism in Bangladesh.*

Chapter 18 (Conclusions: Integration of Efforts): This chapter summarizes the intervention plans and calls for a four-pronged strategy to integrate efforts. These include:

- *Role of National Coordination Bodies*: policy directions from national coordinating bodies such as the National Committee for Security Affairs, National Committee for Intelligence Coordination, and National Committee for Militancy Resistance and Prevention.
- *Inter-Ministerial Coordination*: The Ministry of Home Affairs will take the lead but must coordinate its efforts with other line ministries. The list includes the Ministry of Agriculture, Ministry of Commerce, Ministry of Cultural Affairs, Ministry of Education, Ministry of Labour and Employment, Ministry of Religious Affairs, Ministry of Youth and Sports, and Ministry of Women and Children Affairs.
- *Coordination Among Actors*: Coordination among various counter-terrorism agencies and the prison authorities will be needed.
- *Knowledge Sharing*: Finally, a virtual Knowledge Hub platform can be created to exchange national and international best practices.

In conclusion, this Handbook is the first in South Asia to mainstream deradicalization and rehabilitation in the C/PVE strategy. There is a strong political will among senior government officials and CT agencies to adopt the Handbook as a basis for guiding intervention plans by various actors. The prison authorities and other actors have also shown tremendous support for adopting such a Handbook. Transforming such commitment and enthusiasm into a sustained action is now a call of time. As Bangladesh embarks on implementing a structured plan for the deradicalization and rehabilitation of VEOs, it will need to continuously upgrade the Handbook in light of lessons learned, independent evaluation, and international best practices.

Contents

1 **Introduction** 1
- 1.1 Context Analysis 1
- 1.2 Why Deradicalization and Rehabilitation Matters 1
- 1.3 Core Principles 3
- 1.4 Key Terms 3
- 1.5 Target Audience 4
- 1.6 How to Use this Handbook 5
- References 6

Part I Preparatory Stage

2 **Target Beneficiaries** 11
- 2.1 Introduction 11
- 2.2 Typology of Beneficiaries 11
- 2.3 Profiles of Arrested VEOs 15
- 2.4 Profiles of At-Risk Communities 17
- 2.5 The Settings 18
- 2.6 Conclusion 18
- References 19

3 **Key Actors** 21
- 3.1 Introduction 21
- 3.2 Law Enforcement and Intelligence Agencies 21
- 3.3 Prison Authorities 23
- 3.4 Forensic Psychologists and Clinical Psychologists 23
- 3.5 Religious Counsellors 24
- 3.6 Educational Institutions 24
- 3.7 Vocational Skills Trainers 25
- 3.8 Cultural Organizations 25
- 3.9 Social Workers 26

3.10 Business Chambers 26
3.11 Families of VEOs and Victims 27
3.12 Civil Society Organizations (CSO) 27
3.13 Community Gatekeepers/Village Panchayat 28
3.14 Political Actors 28
3.15 Mainstream and Social Media 28
3.16 Conclusion 29
Reference 29

4 Capacity Building of Prison Staff and CT Professionals 31
4.1 Introduction 31
4.2 Desired Outcome 31
4.3 Key Actors 31
4.4 Key Activities 32
4.5 Methods of Operation 33
4.6 Risks and Opportunities 34
4.7 Monitoring and Evaluation Framework 35
4.8 Conclusion 35
References 35

5 Screening and Admission for Assessing Readiness 37
5.1 Introduction 37
5.2 Desired Outcome 37
5.3 Key Actors 38
5.4 Key Activities 38
5.5 Methods of Operation 40
5.6 Risks and Opportunities/Mitigation Strategies 41
5.7 Monitoring and Evaluation Framework 42
5.8 Conclusion 42
References 46

Part II Deradicalization

6 Religious Counselling 49
6.1 Introduction 49
6.2 Desired Outcome 49
6.3 Key Actors 49
6.4 Key Activities 50
6.5 Methods of Operations 52
6.6 Risks and Opportunities 53
6.7 Monitoring and Evaluation Framework 54
6.8 Conclusion 54
References 55

7 Psychological Intervention 57
7.1 Introduction 57
7.2 Desired Outcome 57
7.3 Key Actors 58
7.4 Key Activities 59
7.5 Methods of Operation 61
7.6 Risks and Opportunities 63
7.7 Monitoring and Evaluation Framework 63
7.8 Conclusion 64
References 64

8 Cultural Orientation 65
8.1 Introduction 65
8.2 Desired Outcome 65
8.3 Key Actors 66
8.4 Key Activities 67
8.5 Methods of Operations 68
8.6 Risks and Opportunities/Mitigation Strategies 69
8.7 Monitoring and Evaluation Framework 70
8.8 Conclusion 70
References 70

9 Social Harmony, Pluralism, and Tolerance Through Education 71
9.1 Introduction 71
9.2 Desired Outcome 72
9.3 Key Actors 72
9.4 Key Activities 72
9.5 Methods of Operation 73
9.6 Risks and Opportunities/Mitigation Strategies 74
9.7 Monitoring and Framework 74
9.8 Conclusions 75
References 75

10 Legal Counselling 77
10.1 Introduction 77
10.2 Desired Outcome of Legal Counselling of VEOs 77
10.3 Key Actors 77
10.4 Key Activities 78
10.5 Methods of Operation 79
10.6 Risks and Opportunities/Mitigation Strategies 80
10.7 M&E Framework 80
10.8 Conclusions 81
References 81

Part III Rehabilitation

11 Physical Disengagement 85
11.1 Introduction 85
11.2 Desired Outcome 85
11.3 Key Actors 86
11.4 Key Activities 87
11.5 Methods of Operation 87
11.6 Risk and Opportunities 88
11.7 Monitoring and Evaluation Framework 89
11.8 Conclusion 90
References 90

12 Academic Training 91
12.1 Introduction 91
12.2 Desired Outcome 91
12.3 Key Actors 92
12.4 Key Activities 93
12.5 Methods of Operation 94
12.6 Risks and Opportunities 95
12.7 Monitoring and Evaluation Framework 95
12.8 Conclusions 96
References 96

13 Vocational Skills Training 97
13.1 Introduction 97
13.2 Desired Outcomes 97
13.3 Key Actors 97
13.4 Key Activities 98
13.5 Methods of Operations 98
13.6 Risks and opportunities/Mitigation strategies 99
13.6.1 Monitoring and Evaluation Framework 99
13.7 Conclusion 100
References 100

14 Employment and Entrepreneurial Support 101
14.1 Introduction 101
14.2 Desired Outcome 101
14.3 Key Actors 102
14.4 Key Activities 102
14.5 Methods of Operation 103
14.6 Risks and Opportunities/Mitigation Strategies 104
14.7 Monitoring and Evaluation Framework 104
14.8 Conclusion 105
References 107

15 Support for the Family and Community Members ... 109
15.1 Introduction ... 109
15.2 Desired Outcome ... 109
15.3 Key Actors ... 109
15.4 Key Activities ... 111
15.5 Methods of Operation ... 112
15.6 Risks and Opportunities ... 114
15.6.1 Monitoring and Evaluation Framework ... 114
15.7 Conclusion ... 115
References ... 115

16 Resettlement Support ... 117
16.1 Introduction ... 117
16.2 Desired Outcome ... 117
16.3 Key Actors ... 118
16.4 Key Activities ... 118
16.5 Methods of Operations ... 119
16.6 Risks and Opportunities ... 121
16.7 Monitoring and Evaluation Framework ... 121
16.8 Conclusion ... 122
References ... 122

Part IV Policy Issues

17 Policy Reforms ... 125
17.1 Introduction ... 125
17.2 Desired Outcome ... 125
17.3 Key Actors ... 126
17.4 Key Activities ... 126
17.5 Methods of Operation ... 127
17.6 Risks and Opportunities/Mitigation Strategies ... 128
17.7 Monitoring and Evaluation Framework ... 128
17.8 Conclusion ... 129
References ... 129

18 Conclusions: Integration of Efforts ... 131
18.1 Introduction ... 131
18.2 Summary of Chapters ... 132
18.3 Integration of Efforts ... 134
18.4 Future Directions ... 135

On the Authors ... 137

Abbreviations

ABT	Ansarullah Bangla Team
ATU	Anti-Terrorism Unit
BARD	Bangladesh Academy for Rural Development
BASIS	Bangladesh Association for Software and Information Services
BGMEA	Bangladesh Garment Manufacturers and Exporters Association
BKMEA	Bangladesh Knitwear Manufacturers Association
BKSP	Bangladesh Krira Shikkha Protishtan
BRAC	Building Resources Across Communities
C/PVE	Countering and Preventing Violent Extremism
CAMPE	Campaign for Popular Education
CHT	Chittagong Hill Tracts
CSOs	Civil Society Organizations
CT	Counter Terrorism
CTIB	Counter Terrorism Intelligence Bureau
CTTC	Counter Terrorism and Transnational Crime
CTW	Counter Terrorism Wing
DGFI	Directorate General of Forces Intelligence
FBCCI	Federation of Bangladesh Chambers of Commerce and Industries
HQ	Headquarters
HR	Human Resources
HUJI-B	Harkat ul Jihad al Islami Bangladesh
IID	Institute for Informatics and Development
ISIS	Islamic State of Iraq and Syria
JMB	Jamaat-ul Mujahideen Bangladesh
JSC	Junior School Certificate
LEAs	Law Enforcement Agencies
MARNA	Militant Activity Risks and Needs Assessment
MJF	Manusher Jonno Foundation
MOC	Ministry of Commerce
MoCA	Ministry of Cultural Affairs
MOHA	Ministry of Home Affairs

MOLE	Ministry of Labor and Employment
MORA	Ministry of Religious Affairs
MOSW	Ministry of Social Welfare
MOWCA	Ministry of Women and Children Affairs
MOYS	Ministry of Youth and Sports
NGOs	Non-governmental Organizations
NSI	National Security Intelligence
NTMC	National Telecommunication Monitoring Cell
POC	Person of Concern
PSC	Primary School Certificate
PVE	Preventing Violent Extremism
RAB	Rapid Action Battalion
RRG	Religious Rehabilitation Group
SB	Special Branch
SHED	Secondary and Higher Education Division
SMEs	Small and Medium-Sized Enterprises
SPJ	Structured Professional Judgement
SSC	Secondary School Certificate
TMED	Technical and Madrasah Education Division
TTCs	Technical Training Centers
TVET	Technical and Vocational Training
UNAFEI	UN Asia and Far East Institute for the Prevention of Crime and the Treatment of Offenders
UNICRI	UN Interregional Crime and Justice Research Institute
UNODC	United Nations Office on Drugs and Crime
VDP	Village Defence Party
VE	Violent Extremism
VEOs	Violent Extremist Offenders

List of Figures

Fig. 1.1 Various stages of VEO deradicalization and rehabilitation 5
Fig. 2.1 Key issues under consideration for target beneficiary selection 12
Fig. 2.2 VEO profile indicators 15
Fig. 3.1 List of key actors in VEO deradicalization and rehabilitation 22
Fig. 7.1 Activities and processes in the proposed deradicalization program 61

Chapter 1
Introduction

1.1 Context Analysis

This Handbook for the deradicalization and rehabilitation of violent extremist offenders (VEOs) is developed in the context of rising threats of terrorism posed by a wide variety of violent extremist (VE) groups. Some VE groups have existed for decades, but others have emerged recently. While the ethno-nationalist and the extreme-left groups have long dominated the threat landscape, the faith-based groups have gained some prominence since the late 1990s thanks to patronization by some mainstream political parties opposed to the ideology of secularism and religious harmony (Ahmed and Islam 2021, 2022, 2023; Braithwaite and D'Costa 2018; Amin 1986; Banerjee 1982; Eva and Khan 2018; Jahan 2014; Maniruzzaman 1975). Even within the cohort of faith-based extremism, the perpetrators have chosen various targets and employed diverse tactics (Table 1.1). Some of the terrorist attacks have thus deliberately targeted the rich cultural heritage of Bangladesh or the torchbearers of Bangladesh's pluralistic politics. Others have wanted to attack a foreign diplomat or create panic and fear throughout the country by distributing pamphlets challenging the logic of the democratic system (Ashraf and Islam 2023). The most recent brands of faith-based VE groups have targeted online activists and foreigners with sharply divergent goals.

1.2 Why Deradicalization and Rehabilitation Matters

Deradicalization and rehabilitation are valuable tools for countering and preventing violent extremism (C/PVE) (Altier et al. 2014; Boucek 2008; Bryans 2016). While deradicalization practices aim at cognitive and behavioral transformation among VEOs, rehabilitation strategies promote their social reintegration. They are essential in creating an inclusive, peaceful, and tolerant society (GCTF 2011, 2012, 2015;

I. Ahmed et al., *Handbook on Deradicalization and Rehabilitation of Violent Extremist Offenders in Bangladesh*, SpringerBriefs in Environment, Security, Development and Peace 41, https://doi.org/10.1007/978-3-031-85807-9_1

Table 1.1: Some high-profile terrorist attacks in Bangladesh

Date	Attack target and tactic	Goal	Perpetrator
14 April 2001	Grenade attack on Ramna Batomool Bangla New Year Celebration	Threaten the Bengali culture and heritage	Harkat ul Jihad al Islami (HUJI)-Bangladesh
21 May 2004	Grenade attack on UK High Commissioner to Bangladesh Anwar Chowdhury	To take revenge on UK's support for the U.S.-led Iraq War	Harkat ul Jihad al Islami (HUJI)-Bangladesh
21 August 2004	Grenade attack on Awami League Rally	Assassinate then Opposition Leader Sheikh Hasina and threaten secular political culture	Harkat ul Jihad al Islami (HUJI)-Bangladesh
17 August 2005	Country-wide crude bomb explosion	Create panic and fear throughout the country and challenge democratic system of governance	Jamaat-ul Mujahideen Bangladesh (JMB)
26 February 2015	Knife attack on blogger and online activist Avijit Roy	Take revenge against those who are seen as infidels	Ansarullah Bangla Team (ABT)
1 July 2016	Attack with assault rifles, bombs, pistols, and knives on Foreign visitors of an upscale restaurant Holey Artisan Bakery at the diplomatic zone of Dhaka	Draw international media attention by claiming linkage with an international terrorist network Islamic State of Iraq and Syria (ISIS)	Neo-JMB

Gunaratna and Hasan 2015; Hansen and Lid 2020; Holmer and Shtuni 2017; Horgan and Braddock 2009).

Bangladesh's syncretic values and culture reflect a unique blend of religious and cultural influences and have played an essential role in shaping the country's civilizational heritage. Hence, a critical purpose of adopting a wide range of measures to deradicalize and rehabilitate VEOs is to project Bangladesh's civilizational roots.

The Sylhet division in northeastern Bangladesh provides a valuable case study. Sylhet has consistently recorded the lowest number of violent incidents in Bangladesh. For historians and sociologists, this low record of VE activities in Sylhet can be attributed to its rich tradition of inter-faith and cross-cultural interactions. Sylhet is situated at the crossroads of ancient trade routes. It has a long history of syncretic values and practices influenced by a mix of Hinduism, Buddhism, and Islam. The shrine of Shah Jalal offers a stark example. Shahjalal was a Sufi saint venerated by people from all walks of life and religious traditions. Hence, people from various backgrounds visit the shrine, seek eternal blessings, and offer prayers for the Saint and themselves.

1.3 Core Principles

The core principles of deradicalization and rehabilitation are:

- *Gender sensitivity*: There is a growing trend of women's involvement in VE groups in Bangladesh and worldwide. Hence, this Handbook considers both men and women VEOs as potential beneficiaries of deradicalization and rehabilitation services.
- *Respect for human rights and* the rule of law: Concerned actors and stakeholders involved in implementing this Handbook must comply with international human rights law and humanitarian laws. The legal and policy framework for VEO rehabilitation in Bangladesh must refer to domestic and international human rights norms. For the imprisoned VEOs, some norms relate to access to families and contact with the outside world, the right to legal representation, and freedom of religion.
- *Safety and security of the deradicalization and rehabilitation beneficiaries*: The safety and security of the participants in the VEO deradicalization and rehabilitation program must be ensured. A small group of VEOs may not be willing to join such programs, and they may pose a security risk to those who will participate. Hence, there should be periodic reviews of the physical safety of VEO rehabilitation participants (Ashraf 2021; Bashar 2011; Biswas 2021);
- *Inter-agency coordination*: This Handbook adopts a whole-of-society approach. It maps various actors involved in the deradicalization and rehabilitation of VEOs in Bangladesh. Success will depend on inter-agency and inter-ministerial coordination.
- *Importance of high-quality intelligence*: High-quality intelligence will play an essential role in various stages of implementing this Handbook. Depending on their territorial jurisdiction and mandates, security and intelligence agencies will assess the risks of target beneficiaries and determine the eligibility of participants. They will maintain close contact with the prison's intelligence to determine the risks of prison-based VEOs in the pre-trial, conviction, and pre-release stages (Bryans 2016; Dean et al. 2018; Dreisinger 2016; ERA 2017; IIJ 2015).
- *Monitoring and evaluation:* Independent evaluators must be involved in various stages of the rehabilitative strategy to conduct an impact assessment and generate valuable lessons learned (Cherney 2020).

1.4 Key Terms

Violent extremism refers to holding radical views and turning them into actions for advancing economic, political, or social goals. The primary aim of violent extremism is to create fear and panic among the general public and to exert pressure on a particular government or society to seek concessions for political, ideological, or religious purposes. The term is often used synonymously with terrorism. Violet extremism involves various operational tactics, including bombings, stabbings, mass shootings, hostage-taking, cyber-attacks, and other violent acts (Hoffman 2017; Borum 2011; UNGA 2006).

Violent extremist offenders (VEOs) have been radicalized into violent extremism and have either supported or committed an extremist cause or have participated in the planning and execution of a terrorist attack. They can be members of any homegrown VE groups or inspired by or affiliated with a regional/transnational terrorist network such as Al Qaeda and ISIS (Rabasa et al. 2010; Schuurman et al. 2018)

Radicalization is a process by which individuals or groups adopt extreme political, religious, and social beliefs and values significantly different from those of mainstream society (Borum 2011). This process involves a shift in attitudes and behaviours that can increase the willingness to use or support violence to reach a specific political or ideological objective. Radicalization can involve multiple social, economic, and psychological factors (Kruglanski et al. 2014).

Deradicalization is the process of disengaging individuals from extremist ideologies and preventing them from engaging in violent or terrorist activities (Koehler 2017). It involves identifying the root causes of radicalization and addressing them through psychological, social, and ideological interventions (Silke et al. 2021; Silke and Veldhuis 2017; Sukabdi 2015, 2017; Rabasa et al. 2010)

Rehabilitation is a process through which an individual lives an everyday life after receiving a wide range of services. A successful rehabilitation program means that VEOs have cognitively transformed and have refrained from further engaging in terrorist activities and are thus no longer posing a risk to themselves and society (GCTF 2012; Hettiarachchi 2015; Mullins 2010; Neumann 2010; Uhlmann 2021).

1.5 Target Audience

This Handbook adopts a whole-of-society approach and targets various stakeholders in Bangladesh's government, private sector, and civil society. Policymakers and legislators can review this to determine their roles in addressing the legal and policy vacuum. Various law enforcement and intelligence agencies and the prison authority will find this Handbook helpful in guiding their staff training and regular operations. Among the law enforcement agencies, the Anti Terrorism Unit (ATU), the Counter Terrorism and Transnational Crime (CTTC) Unit of Dhaka Metropolitan Police, and the Rapid Action Battalion (RAB) have taken several ad hoc deradicalization initiatives. This Handbook will provide a valuable toolkit to shape their soft approaches to C/PVE. The prison authority in Bangladesh lacks any programs for VEO rehabilitation. This Handbook will be handy for the Prisons headquarters, the High-Security Prison Unit, and district-level and central prison units currently housing VEOs. As discussed in this document, private entrepreneurs have a role to play in the economic reintegration of VEOs. International development partners interested in capacity building and security sector reforms in Bangladesh will find this Handbook useful.

On the other hand, families and local communities would play a critical role in social reintegration. Finally, educational institutions and psychological and religious counsellors are essential for deradicalization and rehabilitation. They will also find this Handbook helpful in understanding the gaps in current practices and the scope for further improvement.

1.6 How to Use this Handbook

This Handbook can be a policy toolkit and a practitioner's guide. It has four broad parts (Fig. 1.1).

- Preparatory stage
- Deradicalization
- Rehabilitation
- Policy Issues

First, the preparatory stage identifies target beneficiaries of deradicalization, rehabilitation, and critical implementing actors. It then moves on to the screening and

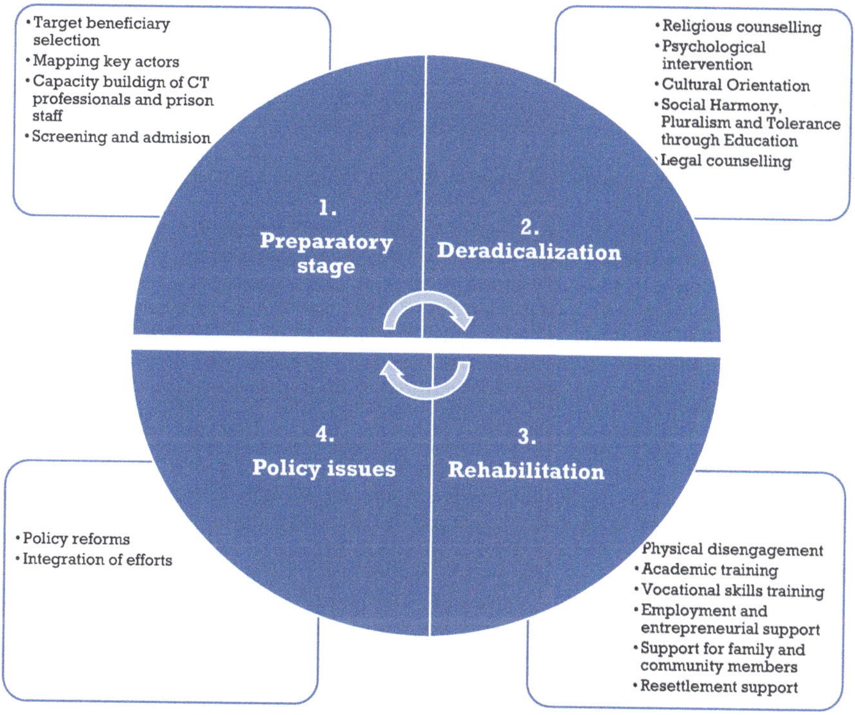

Fig. 1.1 Various stages of VEO deradicalization and rehabilitation

admission process to assess the readiness of target participants and build the capacity of CT professionals and prison staff.

Second, this Handbook will provide a detailed list of deradicalization activities comprising various interventions such as psychological counselling, religious counselling, physical disengagement, and legal counselling.

Third, it focuses on rehabilitation strategies for functional integration and social integration. These strategies include education and skills training, vocational training, employment, and entrepreneurial support. The roles of families and community members, resettlement support, and cultural orientation follow.

Finally, the Handbook discusses legal and policy reforms and preventive deradicalization of indoctrinated VEOs. It concludes with a discussion of integrating approaches.

References

Ahmed, Imtiaz and Monirul Islam, eds. 2023. *Social Stability in Bangladesh: Do Trends Matter?* Dhaka: Centre for Genocide Studies, University of Dhaka and Counter Terrorism & Transnational Crime, Bangladesh Police, January.

Ahmed, Imtiaz and Monirul Islam, eds. 2022. *Preventing Terror Communication in Bangladesh.* Dhaka: Centre for Genocide Studies, University of Dhaka and Counter Terrorism & Transnational Crime, Bangladesh Police, October.

Ahmed, Imtiaz and Monirul Islam, eds. 2021. *Ensuring Life without Terror: Responses to Terrorism in Bangladesh*, two volumes. Dhaka: The University Press Limited.

Altier, Mary Beth, Christian N. Thoroughgood, and John G. Horgan. 2014. "Turning away from terrorism: Lessons from psychology, sociology, and criminology." *Journal of Peace Research* 51 (52): 647–661.

Amin, Md Nurul. 1986. "Maoism in Bangladesh: The Case of the East Bengal Sarbohara Party." *Asian Survey*: 759–773.

Ashraf, ASM Ali. 2021. "A Strategy for the Rehabilitation and Reintegration of Violent Extremist Offenders in Bangladesh." Essay. In Imtiaz Ahmed and Monirul Islam, eds., *Ensuring Life without Terror: Responses to Terrorism in Bangladesh*, The University Press Limited 2,2:11–82.

Ashraf, ASM Ali, and Islam, Mohamed Saiful. 2023. Islamist Militant Groups and Crime-Terror Nexus in Bangladesh. *Studies in Conflict and Terrorism*, 46 (9): 1678–1701. https://www.tandfonline.com/doi/full/https://doi.org/10.1080/1057610X.2020.1868099.

Banerjee, Sumanta. 1982. "Bangladesh's Marxist-Leninists: I." *Economic and Political Weekly* 1982: 1267–1271.

Bashar, Iftekharul. 2011. "Bangladesh's Forgotten Crisis: land, ethnicity, and violence in the Chittagong Hill Tracts." *Counter Terrorist Trends and Analyses* 3 (4): 1–5.

Biswas, Niloy Ranjan. 2021. Rehabilitation of Ex-Terrorists and their Role in Counter Terrorism. In Imtiaz Ahmed and Monirul Isam, eds. *Ensuring Life Without Terror: Responses to Terrorism in Bangladesh.* Dhaka: University Press Limited, 83–163.

Borum, Randy. 2011. "Radicalization into Violent Extremism I: A Review of Social Science Theories." *Journal of Strategic Security* 4 (4): 7–36. https://doi.org/10.5038/1944-0472.4.4.1.

Boucek, Christopher. 2008. *Saudi Arabia's" Soft" Counterterrorism Strategy: Prevention, Rehabilitation, and Aftercare.* Washington, DC: Carnegie Endowment for International Peace. Vol. 97.

Braithwaite, John, and Bina D'Costa. *Cascades of Violence: War, Crime, and Peacebuilding Across South Asia.* ANU Press, 2018.

Bryans, Shane. 2016. CRIMINAL JUSTICE HANDBOOK SERIES *UNODC Handbook on the Management of Violent Extremist Prisoners and the Prevention of Radicalization to Violence in Prisons*. https://www.unodc.org/pdf/criminal_justice/Handbook_on_VEPs.pdf.

Cherney, Adrian. 2020. "Evaluating interventions to disengage extremist offenders: a study of the proactive, integrated support model (PRISM)." *Behavioral Sciences of Terrorism and Political Aggression* 12 (1): 17–36.

Dean, Chris, Monica Lloyd, Carys Keane, Beverly Powis, and Kiran Randhawa. 2018. *Intervening with Extremist Offenders – A Pilot Study*. HM Prison and Probation Service. London: UK Home Office.

Dreisinger, Baz. 2016. *Incarceration Nations: A Journey to Justice in Prisons around the World*. New York: Other Press.

ERA (Academy of European Law). 2017. Preventing Radicalisation in Detention. Presented in Vienna, 12–13 October.

Eva, Shahabanu, and Tareq Hossain Khan. 2018. "Preventing Violence and Sustaining Peace in Post-Conflict Society: A Study of Chittagong Hill Tracts Peace Accord." *Asian Studies: Jahangir Nagar University Journal of Government and Politics* 37.

Global Counterterrorism Forum (GCTF). 2011. *The Rabat Memorandum on Good Practices for Effective Counterterrorism Practice in the Criminal Justice Sector. Criminal Justice Sector/Rule of Law Working Group*. The Hague: GCTF.

Global Counterterrorism Forum (GCTF). 2012. *Rome Memorandum on Good Practices for Rehabilitation and Reintegration of Violent Extremist Offenders*. The Hague: GCTF.

Global Counterterrorism Forum (GCTF). 2015. *Initiative to Address the Life Cycle of Radicalization to Violence: Addendum to the Rome Memorandum on Good Practices for Rehabilitation and Reintegration of Violent Extremist Offenders*. The Hague: GCTF.

Gunaratna, and Mohamed Feisal Bin Mohamed Hassan. 2015. "Terrorist rehabilitation: the Singapore experience." In Gunaratna, Rohan and Mohamed Bin Ali (eds.). *Terrorist rehabilitation: A new frontier in counter-terrorism*. Singapore: Imperial College Press, pp. 1–20.

Hansen, S.J., and Lid, S. (Eds.). (2020). *Routledge Handbook of Deradicalisation and Disengagement (1st ed.)*. Routledge. https://doi.org/10.4324/9781315387420.

Hettiarachchi, Malkanthi. 2015. "Sri Lanka's Rehabilitation Programme: The humanitarian mission two." In Gunaratna, Rohan and Mohamed Bin Ali (eds.). *Terrorist rehabilitation: A new frontier in counter-terrorism*. Singapore: Imperial College Press, pp. 103–131.

Hoffman, Bruce. 2017. *Inside Terrorism*. 3rd ed. New York: Columbia University Press.

Holmer, Georgia, and Adrian Shtuni. 2017. *Returning Foreign Fighters and the Reintegration Imperative*. United States Institute of Peace (USIP) Special Report. Washington, DC: USIP.

Horgan, John, and Kurt Braddock. 2009. *Assessing the Effectiveness of Current De-Radicalization Initiatives and Identifying Implications for the Development of U.S.-Based Initiatives in Multiple Settings*. Washington, DC: National Consortium for the Study of Terrorism and Responses to Terrorism (START).

Jahan, Rounaq. 2014. "Political parties in Bangladesh." *Centre for Policy Dialogue (CPD)-Chartered Management Institute (CMI) Working Paper series*. Dhaka: CPD.

Koehler, D. 2017. *Understanding Deradicalization: Methods, Tools, and Programs for Countering Violent Extremism*. London and New York: Routledge.

Kruglanski, A.W., Gelfand, M.J., Bélanger, J.J., Sheveland, A., Hetiarachchi, M. and Gunaratna, R. (2014), Processes of Radicalization and Deradicalization. Political Psychology, 35: 69–93. https://doi.org/10.1111/pops.12163.

Maniruzzaman, Talukder. 1975. "Bangladesh: an unfinished revolution?" *The Journal of Asian Studies* 34 (4): 891–911.

Mullins, Sam. 2010. "Rehabilitation of Islamist terrorists: Lessons from criminology." *Dynamics of Asymmetric Conflict* 3 (3): 162–193.

Neumann, Peter R. 2010. *International Centre for the Study of Radicalisation and Political Violence (ICSR) Prisons and Terrorism: Radicalisation and De-Radicalisation in 15 Countries*. https://www.clingendael.org/sites/default/files/pdfs/Prisons-and-terrorism-15-countries.pdf.

Rabasa, A., Pettyjohn, S. L., Ghez, J. J., & Boucek, C. (2010). Deradicalizing Islamist extremists. RAND Corp Arlington VA National Security Research Div. https://www.rand.org/content/dam/rand/pubs/monographs/2010/RAND_MG1053.sum.pdf.

Schuurman, Bart, Edwin Bakker, and Quirine Eijkman. 2018. "Structural Influences on Involvement in European Homegrown Jihadism: A Case Study." *Terrorism and Political Violence* 30 (1): 97–115.

Silke, A., Morrison, J., Maiberg, H., Slay, C., and Stewart, R. (2021). The Phoenix model of disengagement and deradicalization from terrorism and violent extremism. *Monatsschrift für Kriminologie und Strafrechtsreform, 104*(3), 310–320.

Silke, Andrew, and Tinka Veldhuis. 2017. "Countering Violent Extremism in Prisons: A review of key recent research and critical research gaps." *Perspectives on Terrorism* 11 (5): 2–11.

Sukabdi, Z. A. 2015. "A Review on Rehabilitation and Deradicalization." *Journal of Terrorism Research* 6: 35–56.

Sukabdi, Zora A. 2017. "Psychological rehabilitation for ideology-based terrorism offenders." *International Journal of Neurorehabilitation* 4 (1): 1–9.

The International Institute for Justice and the Rule of Law (IIJ). 2015. *Prison Management Recommendations to Counter and Address Prison Radicalization.* Valletta: IIJ.

Uhlmann, Milena. 2021. *BMI-Strategic Enhancement of Deradicalisation/Disengagement Approaches within a Comprehensive Framework of Preventing and Countering Violent Islamist Extremism and Violent Right-Wing Extremism.* https://www.bmi.bund.de/SharedDocs/downloads/EN/publikationen/2021/strategic-enhancement-deradicalisation.pdf?__blob=publicationFile&v=5.

United Nations General Assembly. 2006. *Resolution adopted by the General Assembly on 8 September 2006: 60/288. The United Nations Global Counter-Terrorism Strategy.* New York: UNGA.

Part I
Preparatory Stage

Chapter 2
Target Beneficiaries

2.1 Introduction

This chapter contends that Bangladesh should adopt a comprehensive and inclusive strategy for the deradicalization and rehabilitation of VEOs. Such a strategy will consider four issues: the legal-judicial status of VEOs, their ideological predispositions, their profiles, and the setting in which deradicalization and rehabilitation services will be offered (Fig. 2.1). On the first issue, this Handbook applies to VEOs maintaining any of the following legal-judicial statuses: (a) convicted and imprisoned; (b) convicted but released after prison term; (c) under-trial detainees; (d) under-trial on bail; (e) surrendered but not imprisoned; and (f) at-risk communities. Secondly, the beneficiary list would include VEOs affiliated with or inspired by any of the three ideological groups: faith-based militancy, left-wing extremism, and ethno-nationalist insurgency (to understand the emergence of left-wing extremism in Bangladesh, read: Mohaiemen 2006; Sarkar 2015). Third, this long list of target beneficiaries will receive deradicalization and rehabilitation services in prison settings or at the local community level (Veldhuis 2012; Walkenhorst et al. 2020; Morton and Siber 2018). Convicted VEOs who are yet to finish their prison terms and under-trial detainees who have not received bail will receive services at the prisons. At the same time, the rest can be eligible to receive rehabilitative services at the community level.

2.2 Typology of Beneficiaries

(a) Convicted and imprisoned VEOs

The term 'convicted VEOs' refers to VEOs who have received jail terms or death sentences in one or more terrorism cases. Approximately 300 faith-based VEOs in Bangladesh have received various convictions, with only a few convicted to death

I. Ahmed et al., *Handbook on Deradicalization and Rehabilitation of Violent Extremist Offenders in Bangladesh*, SpringerBriefs in Environment, Security, Development and Peace 41, https://doi.org/10.1007/978-3-031-85807-9_2

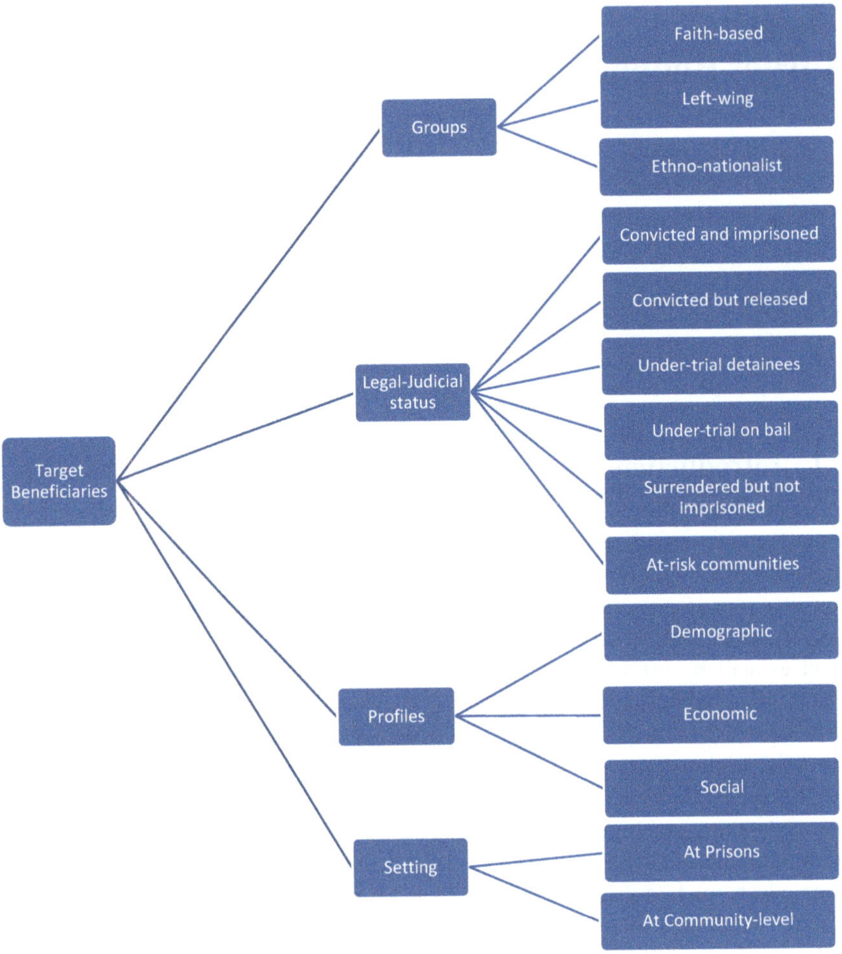

Fig. 2.1 Key issues under consideration for target beneficiary selection

sentences. There is no data on convicted left-wing and ethno-nationalist VEOs. Expert opinion suggests that the number of these latter two categories would not be more than two dozen VEOs.

The convicted VEOs are assessed as high-risk offenders and housed in a high-security prison cell. In contrast to ordinary VEO foot soldiers, they have a proven record of involvement in terrorist attacks. Such involvement may range from training VEOs, funding VE operations, maintaining VE propaganda, managing liaisons with domestic and transnational VE networks, and carrying out VE attacks (UK Ministry of Justice 2019; Sumpter 2018, 2019)

The convicts receiving death sentences may get some counseling but not for rehabilitation purposes. If they confess their crimes and become remorseful, they can convey to other prison inmates that involvement in VE is a wrongful and punishable act. However, the ideal candidate for prison-based deradicalization and rehabilitation programs would be VEOs receiving various jail terms. The main goal is to ensure that regardless of their involvement in faith-based militancy, left-wing extremism, or ethno-nationalist rebellion, they deserve a second chance before returning to their families and communities (Stys et al. 2016).

(b) Post-release VEOs

Post-release VEOs constitute a cohort of convicted VEOs who have already been released from prison after finishing their terms or have been acquitted of a case. They are no longer in jail because there are no pending cases against them. Among the faith-based VEOs who have left the prison after finishing terms, only a few of them or their families have received some cash incentives from CT agencies as part of a deradicalization and economic rehabilitation effort, and the number will not exceed 30. Post-release VEOs are also ideal candidates for VEO deradicalization and rehabilitation, so they do not re-engage in VE groups (Jacobson 2010).

(c) Under-trial Detainee VEOs

Under-trial detainees constitute an essential group of target beneficiaries for VEO deradicalization and rehabilitation. There are approximately 400 under-trial detainees in Bangladeshi prisons. They are accused in terrorism cases and are awaiting a verdict. Some under-trial detainees are in the pre-trial stage, which means that police investigations still need to be completed, and hence, a final police report (also known as a charge sheet) is pending. For other under-trial detainees, a final police report has been submitted, and the trial is ongoing. While the convicts may be willing to participate in a deradicalization and rehabilitation program, under-trial detainees may be unwilling to attend such programs, fearing this may affect the status of their trial case. In such cases, the benefits and implications of prison-based disengagement and rehabilitation programs must be communicated to the under-trial detainee VEOs (Lemisio and Visser 2017).

(d) Under-Trial VEOs on Bail

'Under-trial VEOs on Bail' refers to VEOs currently on bail but awaiting verdicts on one or more terrorism cases. Media reports indicate that in recent years, about 600 faith-based under-trial VEOs got bail in terrorism cases. There is no data on convicted left-wing and ethno-nationalist VEOs. Expert opinion suggests that the number of these latter two categories would be less than 100. In recent years, many left-wing VEOs have surrendered to the Police, and only a few with criminal charges were imprisoned. Like the under-trial detainees in the prisons, the under-trial detainees on bail may only be willing to receive rehabilitative services if they are convinced of the benefits of such programs.

(e) Surrendered but not imprisoned

This category of VEOs includes radicalized individuals who have surrendered to law enforcement agencies but have not been imprisoned for two reasons: either they did not commit any punishable criminal offense or received a general amnesty from the government as part of a broader reconciliation effort (UNSC 2014). There are several instances in which Bangladeshi VEOs from various ideological groups surrendered to the government and were not imprisoned for the above reasons. For example, between 1998 and 2019, at least 2,200 left-wing VEOs surrendered to the Police. As for the ethno-nationalist rebels, about 2,000–3,000 Shanti Bahini rebels surrendered to the government after the 1997 CHT Peace Accord (IWGIA 2012; Kundu et al. 2011). The surrender rate of faith-based VEOs pales in comparison. Between 2016 and 2022, nearly two dozen faith-based VEOs have surrendered to various CT agencies (ATU, CTTC, and RAB). The surrendered VEOs of all three ideological camps received cash incentives from the Government of Bangladesh as part of ad hoc rehabilitation efforts. Some of the surrendered VEOs have also received food stamps (former CHT combatants) or jobs in lower rank posts of Police and Ansar and VDP force (former CHT rebels and left-wing VEOs). However, they have not received comprehensive support, including psycho-social counseling, educational and skills development training, and resettlement services (Panday and Jamil 2015; Alim 2011). It is high time that comprehensive deradicalization and rehabilitation programs cover surrendered VEOs.

(f) At-risk communities

The term 'at-risk communities' broadly refers to three sub-groups of people:

- Those who are vulnerable to radicalization and recruitment into violent extremism.
- Those who are indoctrinated and radicalized but not charged.
- Those who have self-withdrawn from VE activities but are not charged.

None of these three sub-sets of people have been indicted for two reasons: either they have not committed any punishable offence, or the law enforcement agencies need more substantive evidence to accuse them under the applicable anti-terrorism laws.

There must be precise data on the number of individuals living in at-risk communities. A comprehensive deradicalization and rehabilitation program requires identifying vulnerable communities and developing measures to counter extremist propaganda and recruitment drives in such communities. Such programs are broadly defined as PVE programs in which local NGOs and civil society organizations can play an important role. The Habibie Center runs many PVE programs in Indonesia that target at-risk and vulnerable youth. In Bangladesh, the CT agencies (ATU, CTTC, and RAB) have several ongoing outreach programs targeting students of various educational institutions. However, such programs rarely involve psycho-social counseling and are limited to daylong seminars without an impact assessment.

2.3 Profiles of Arrested VEOs

An effective strategy for the deradicalization and rehabilitation of VEOs requires mapping the profiles of arrested VEOs. This section analyzes the profiles of 1,200 faith-based VEOs detained in Bangladesh in various cases between 2001 and 2020. Data for three clusters of indicators are pertinent for discussion (Fig. 2.2).

Among the demographic indicators, the most prominent are age, gender, place of origin, and educational background. First, the arrested VEOs vary in age and academic background. Nearly 40% of them come from the 31–40 age group, 25% from the 21–30 age group, 20% from the 41–50 age group, 10% from the 51–60 age group, and only 5% from the 15–20 age group. Regarding gender, roughly 10–15% of under-trial detainees are women, while the rest are men.

Second, 2% of the VEOs are women who play the role of homemakers. This indicates women are under-represented in faith-based extremism in Bangladesh.

Third, the detainees come from various geographical regions, with the Rajshahi Division dominating the place of origin. Nearly half (49%) of the under-trial detainees are from Rajshahi, 32% from Rangpur, 8% from Mymensingh, 4% from Sylhet, 3% from Dhaka, 2% from Chattogram, 1% from Khulna, 1% from Barisal divisions. More interventions for preventive deradicalization programs would be needed in the Rajshahi and Rangpur divisions.

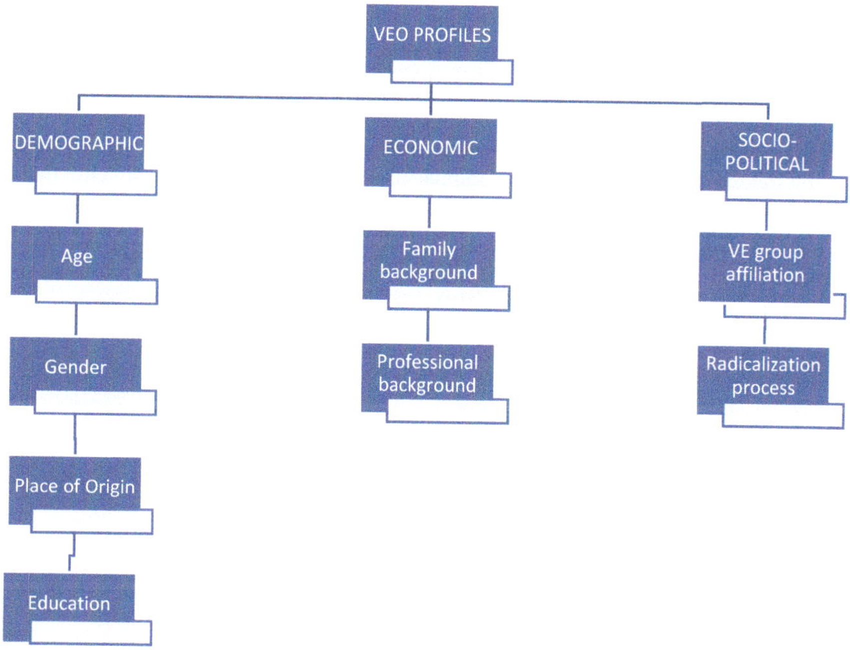

Fig. 2.2 VEO profile indicators

Fourth, when designing educational programs for deradicalization and rehabilitation, one needs to keep in mind a considerable variation among the academic achievements of under-trial VEOs: 70% come from Non-Madrasa (Bangla and English Medium schools) backgrounds, 17% from Madrasas, and the rest of 13% are either illiterate or whose educational achievements are not known. Disaggregated data show that within the non-Madrassa category, 12% have a bachelor's degree, and 4% have a master's degree. Within this same category, 8% finished the 12th grade, 18% the 10th grade, 12% the 8th grade, and 16% the 5th grade. On the other hand, among those with a Madrassa background, only 2% are from the Qawmi Madrassa, and 15% are from the Alia Madrassa.

Family and professional backgrounds are the most important economic indicators. The VEOs report diverse family backgrounds. An overwhelming majority—45%—come from low-income families, 28% from middle-income families, 24% from lower-middle-income families, and only 3% from high-income families.

The diverse professional backgrounds of the VEOs would help design economic rehabilitation and reintegration opportunities; we need to look at the diverse professional backgrounds of the under-trial VEOs. Data suggest that 61% of VEOs come from four categories: 17% are farmers, 15% are businesspeople, 17% are laborers (including 14% day laborers and 3% ready-made garment workers), and 12% are students. Among the under-trial VEOS, 23% are service-holders. This service-holder category includes 6% working in the private sector, 6% serving as non-Madrassa teachers, 5% as Mosque preachers and Madrassa teachers, 4% as doctors (including village doctors, homeopathy doctors), and 2% as engineers. Among the remaining 16% of VEOs, 7% are employed in various jobs (including lawyers, deed writers, and journalists), 7% are unemployed, and 2% are homemakers.

VEO group affiliation and radicalization processes are essential to designing rehabilitation programs among the socio-political indicators. Nearly 60% of the VEOs are members of the old faction of Jamaat'ul Mujahideen Bangladesh (Old-JMB), 10% new faction of JMB (Neo-JMB), 10% of Ansar al Islam (AAI)/Ansarullah Bangla Team (ABT), and the rest are from Allahr Dal, Hizbut Tahrir, and Harkat ul Jihad al Islami Bangladesh (HUJI-B). This disaggregated data would help choose a representative cohort of VEO deradicalization and rehabilitation beneficiaries.

Finally, for community-level preventive interventions, we need to look at the process of radicalization:

- VE group members radicalized 34% through in-person communication.
- 22% were radicalized in the virtual platform.
- 18% were influenced by their social networks comprising peers, family, and friends.

Mosque leaders also acted as radicalizers. Little over 6% of under-trial detainees were influenced by Islamic preachers, including the Mosque Imam, Muazzin, and other Islamic scholars. Left-wing VE groups radicalized a small cohort of 5% of VEOs, and another cohort of 5% of VEOs was self-radicalized.

So far, only the data for faith-based under-trial detainees have been analyzed. No publicly available data exists for under-trial VEOs affiliated with either ultra-left-wing groups [*charampanthi songothon*] or ethno-nationalist groups. Most VEOs in these two categories are widely believed to come from low-income families, mainly aged 21–40, with no more than 10th grade of general education. While a small minority of women have been drawn into faith-based extremism, women are under-represented, mainly in left-wing and ethno-nationalist extremism.

The CT agencies in Bangladesh do not maintain data on the prison population. Hence, there is no disaggregated data on VEOs supporting various legal-judicial statuses, including convicted prison inmates, released VEOs, under-trial detainees, and under-trial on-bail VEOs.

There is no disaggregated data on the profiles of the VEOs on bail, convicted VEOs, and post-release VEOs. In the absence of such disaggregated data, the general profile of the under-trial VEOs should serve as a basis for designing rehabilitative programs for other categories of VEOs. Although various district-level police administrations maintain some data for the surrendered left-wing VEOs, there is no database of surrendered but not imprisoned ethno-nationalist rebels. Data on faith-based VEOs who have surrendered are included in the profiles analyzed here.

2.4 Profiles of At-Risk Communities

There are no publicly accessible data on the profile of at-risk communities. However, the under-trial detainees' profiles would mirror the at-risk population's category. The following attributes of faith-based VEOS are drawn from the preceding discussions and also substantiated by expert opinion:

- Young people in their 20s and 30s in the Rajshahi and Rangpur divisions are more vulnerable to VE recruitment and radicalization (Ahmed and Islam 2021). The puritanist *Ahle Hadith* movement in the greater Rajshahi region appears to be the significant driver of VE groups. While the Dhaka division has produced a small group of VEOs, the leadership structure of AAI and Neo-JMB groups has come from the urban areas of Dhaka. Since the Khulna and Barisal regions have lower penetration of VE groups, the positive factors in these regions must be further studied and drawn into designing P/CVE programs.
- One out of five militants is likely to come from the Madrassa background, while the rest are from general schooling backgrounds (Shaon 2018; Chandan 2017). English medium schools in urban areas are vulnerable to penetration by VE groups. A small section of public and private university students is susceptible to recruitment into AAI and Neo-JMB groups inspired by the global VE networks of Al Qaeda and ISIS (Ashraf and Islam 2023).
- Some young people, while studying abroad, were radicalized by transnational terrorist networks.

- Female radicalization is a new trend. One out of seven militants is likely to be a woman. They are primarily spouses.
- Online radicalization is increasing. One out of five militants is now radicalized in the virtual platform (Ahmed and Islam 2022). The radicalizers now rely on a hybrid communication strategy combining both in-person contacts and virtual communication using secure mobile Apps (Ashraf 2024).
- Only a handful of Bangladeshis reportedly joined ISIS as foreign fighters. There is no precise estimate of how many have joined and how many have returned. One disillusioned Bangladeshi youth who went to Syria to join ISIS returned to Bangladesh and cooperated with the security forces by describing the process through which he was radicalized and the cause of his disillusionment.

2.5 The Settings

Various disengagement and reintegration programs for VEOs will be carried out in two settings: at the prison and community levels. The Bangladeshi prison system has 13 central and 55 district jails (Department of Prisons 2017). VEOs are concentrated in a high-security central jail in the Gazipur district. Hence, the high-security prison unit will be ideal for prison-based deradicalization and rehabilitation programs (Ashraf 2021). As for the community-level VEO rehabilitation program, various outreach and P/CVE programs will be organized at schools, colleges, universities, and madrassahs, targeting the student population. Local CSOs will be partnered to implement grassroots rehabilitation programs. CT agencies (ATU, CTTC, and RAB) may choose to organize some events in their preferred venues.

2.6 Conclusion

This chapter has discussed four critical issues for considering the target beneficiaries of VEO deradicalization and rehabilitation in Bangladesh. First, it argued that the beneficiaries might come from various legal-judicial backgrounds regardless of their arrest, imprisonment, or conviction status. Second, it contends that an inclusive VEO rehabilitation strategy must extend its coverage to VEOs affiliated with various ideological groups. Third, a multi-stakeholder rehabilitation and reintegration strategy for VEOs must consider the target population's demographic, economic, and sociopolitical profiles. Finally, the prisons and local communities will provide two distinct settings for implementing a VEO rehabilitation strategy.

References

Ahmed, Imtiaz and Monirul Islam, eds., *Preventing Terror Communication in Bangladesh*, co-edited (Dhaka: Centre for Genocide Studies, University of Dhaka and Counter Terrorism & Transnational Crime, Bangladesh Police, October 2022).

Ahmed, Imtiaz and Monirul Islam, eds., *Ensuring Life without Terror: Responses to Terrorism in Bangladesh*, two volumes (Dhaka: The University Press Limited, 2021).

Alim, Syed F. 2011. "Left movement in the post-independence era." *The Daily Star* Archive. http://archive.thedailystar.net/suppliments/2011/anniversary/section2/pg11.htm.

Ashraf, ASM Ali. 2021. "A Strategy for the Rehabilitation and Reintegration of Violent Extremist Offenders in Bangladesh." Essay. In Imtiaz Ahmed and Monirul Islam, eds., *Ensuring Life without Terror: Responses to Terrorism in Bangladesh*, The University Press Limited 2,2:11–82.

Ashraf, ASM Ali. 2024. *Exploring Terrorism using Cyberspace: Bangladesh Perspective*. Dhaka: Research Report prepared for Anti Terrorism Unit, Bangladesh Police.

Ashraf, ASM Ali, and Islam, Mohamed Saiful. 2023. Islamist Militant Groups and Crime-Terror Nexus in Bangladesh. *Studies in Conflict and Terrorism*, 46 (9): 1678–1701. https://www.tandfonline.com/doi/full/https://doi.org/10.1080/1057610X.2020.1868099.

Chandan, Md Shahnawaz Khan. 2017. *"Alia Madrasa: An Education System on Its Death Bed."* The Daily Star. https://www.thedailystar.net/star-weekend/alia-madrasa-1482232.

Department of Prisons Bangladesh. Bangladesh Jail. 2017. *Prison Population Statistics*. Dhaka: Department of Prison.

International Work Group for Indigenous Affairs (IWGIA). 2012. *Militarization in the Chittagong Hill Tracts, Bangladesh: The Slow Demise of the Region's Indigenous Peoples*. IWGIA Organising Committee Report No. 14. Copenhagen: IWGIA.

Jacobson, Michael. 2010. *Terrorist Dropouts: Learning from those who have left*. Washington, DC: Washington Institute for Near East Policy.

Kundu, Debasish Kumar, Mrinmoy Samadder, Ashrafuzzaman Khan, and Sharin Shajahan Naomi. 2011. *State of Justice in Chittagong Hill Tracts: Exploring the Formal and Informal Justice Institutions of Indigenous Communities*. Research Monograph Series No. 44. Dhaka: BRAC Centre.

Lemisio, Folole, and Remona Visser. 2017. *Specific Measures: Disengagement Interventions in Prisons*. 167th United Nations Asia and Far East Institute for the Prevention of Crime and the Treatment of Offenders (UNAFEI) International Training Course Visiting Experts' Papers. Resource Material Series No. 104. Tokyo: UNAFEI.

Mohaiemen, Naeem. 2006. "Terrorists or Guerrillas in the Mist." *Sarai Reader*.

Morton, Jesse, and Mitchell D. Siber. *When Terrorists Come Home: The Need for Rehabilitating and Reintegrating America's Convicted Jihadists* (New York: Counter Extremism Project, December 2018).

Panday, Pranab Kumar, and Ishtiaq Jamil. 2015. "Conflict in the Chittagong Hill Tracts of Bangladesh 1: An unimplemented accord and continued violence." In *Ethnic Subnationalist Insurgencies in South Asia*, pp. 143–160. New Delhi: Routledge.

Sarkar, S. 2015. "The role of the left in Bangladesh's democracy: challenges and prospects." In *Democratic Governance and Politics of the Left in South Asia. New Delhi: Aakar Books*, pp. 228-244.

Shaon, Ashif Islam. 2018. *"Why Some Parents Prefer Madrasa to School." Dhaka Tribune.*, 18 January. https://www.dhakatribune.com/bangladesh/bangladesh-others/135780/why-some-parents-prefer-madrasa-to-school.

Stys, Yvonne, Rick McEachran, and Marsha Axford. 2016. *Ways Forward: Applying Lessons Learned in the Management of Radicalized Offenders to Canadian Federal Corrections*. Ottawa: Correctional Service of Canada.

Sumpter, Cameron. 2018. *Returning Indonesian Extremists: Unclear Intentions and Unprepared Responses*. International Centre for Counter-Terrorism (ICCT) Policy Brief. The Hague: ICCT.

Sumpter, Cameron. 2019. *Reintegration in Indonesia: Extremists, Start-ups and Occasional Engagements*. The Hague: International Centre for Counter-Terrorism (ICCT).
UK Ministry of Justice. 2019. *The Structural Properties of the Extremism Risk Guidelines (ERG22+): a structured formulation tool for extremist offenders*. London: Ministry of Justice.
United Nations Security Council (UNSC). 2014. *Resolution 2178 was Adopted by the Security Council at its 7272nd meeting on 24 September 2014*. New York: UNGA.
Veldhuis, Tinka. 2012. *Designing Rehabilitation and Reintegration Programmes for Violent Extremist Offenders: A Realist Approach*. International Centre for Counter-Terrorism (ICCT) Research Paper. The Hague: ICCT.
Walkenhorst, Dennis et al. 2020. *RAN Rehabilitation Manual: Rehabilitation of Radicalised and Terrorist Offenders for First-line Practitioners*. https://home-affairs.ec.europa.eu/system/files/2020-06/ran_rehab_manual_en.pdf.

Chapter 3
Key Actors

3.1 Introduction

This chapter focuses on the actors implementing the deradicalization and rehabilitation of VEOs in Bangladesh. It conducts stakeholder mapping in the context of Bangladesh's experience of countering and preventing violent extremism (C/PVE) (Fig. 3.1). The primary referent objective here is the human being, such as violent extremist offenders (VEOs). Nevertheless, it also considers the significance of relevant state and non-state institutions and their collective strength to prevent violent extremism.

3.2 Law Enforcement and Intelligence Agencies

Deradicalization and rehabilitation of VEOs are crucial components in the broader counter-terrorism activities conducted by law enforcement and intelligence agencies. The role of law enforcement agencies in taking softer counter-terrorism efforts may take multiple forms. They can coordinate with other agencies to plan and implement reintegration programs and to coordinate and evaluate. The following is a list of significant law enforcement and intelligence agencies that will find this Handbook useful for implementing deradicalization and rehabilitation programs:

- Anti Terrorism Unit (ATU)
- Counter Terrorism and Transnational Crime (CTTC) Unit
- Rapid Action Battalion (RAB)

These three agencies have carried out various ad hoc deradicalization and rehabilitation activities and have the competence and the mandate to do these. A brief profile of these three agencies should clearly explain their strength and roles in C/PVE.

I. Ahmed et al., *Handbook on Deradicalization and Rehabilitation of Violent Extremist Offenders in Bangladesh*, SpringerBriefs in Environment, Security, Development and Peace 41, https://doi.org/10.1007/978-3-031-85807-9_3

Fig. 3.1 List of key actors in VEO deradicalization and rehabilitation

Both ATU and CTTC are civilian police units with different territorial jurisdictions. CTTC became operational in 2016 with the twin goals of fighting terrorism and transnational crime, primarily in the Dhaka Metropolitan Police area. It has operated well beyond the DMP area with administrative orders to arrest VEOs, investigate VE activities, and respond to VE threats. The ATU was formed in 2018 as a national unit that operates all over Bangladesh. It has an HQ in Dhaka and divisional-level offices in the country. Both ATU and CTTC have dedicated teams for intelligence, investigation, operations, cybercrime, bomb disposal units, and armed response teams. Each ATU and CTTC has about 600 personnel who can tap the support of any other police units deployed throughout the country.

While ATU and CTTC are civilian police units, the RAB is a paramilitary police unit with personnel drawn from the defense services and civilian police. It was established in 2004 and was vital in arresting the top faith-based VE leaders of HUJI and JMB groups. Its HQ in Dhaka has 15 battalions spread throughout the country.

Intelligence agencies have the expertise to track the VEO's activities and find the information necessary for risk assessment and after-release re-engagement with VEO networks. The following intelligence agencies have dedicated resources for the surveillance of VE groups and are thus well-placed to contribute to the deradicalization and rehabilitation of VEOs:

- Counter Terrorism Intelligence Bureau (CTIB) of Directorate General of Forces Intelligence (DGFI)
- Counter Terrorism Wing (CTW) of National Security Intelligence (NSI)
- Counter Terrorism Section of Special Branch
- National Telecommunication Monitoring Cell (NTMC)
- Lawful Interception Cell of Police Headquarters

3.3 Prison Authorities

The Department of Jail, under the Ministry of Home Affairs, is an essential stakeholder in the deradicalization and rehabilitation of prison-based VEOs. There are currently 68 prisons in Bangladesh—13 Central Jail and 55 District Jail. The prisons hold two types of VEOs: the under-trial and the convicted VEOs. The Kashimpur High-Security Prison Unit has many VEO inmates, while other district-level and central jails have a few. Efforts should be taken to provide capacity building of prison staff so that they are well prepared to manage a wide range of prison-based deradicalization and rehabilitation programs. Initially, the high-security prison staff will receive the training; over time, other prison staff will be included in the capacity-building program.

Since the prison staff can actively monitor the behavior of VEO inmates, the prison authorities can share information with other agencies about imprisoned VEOs to assist in assessing the eligibility of the potential rehabilitation beneficiaries. The Prison authorities must collaborate with different actors to minimize the risk of prison radicalization and new VEO recruitment. Rehabilitation activities need to start for detainees. The prison premises can be a place for rehabilitation interventions where the prison authorities can help by sharing information about the VEOs and collaborating with other actors to provide necessary prison-based interventions. Prison authorities may require support from educators, psychologists, and other specialists to support rehabilitees in offering chances for reintegration. Finally, they can prepare the VEOs for release and plan for prison-based rehabilitation activities.

3.4 Forensic Psychologists and Clinical Psychologists

Forensic psychologists will play a crucial role in conducting the risk assessment of potential VEO rehabilitation beneficiaries to determine their readiness for participating in a deradicalization and rehabilitation program. Once the VEOs are enrolled in a deradicalization program—both at the community level or in the prison setting—clinical psychologists will come to the scene by offering psychotherapy sessions.

A VEO with psychological disorders and impaired psychological functioning may not have the capacity to receive other rehabilitative interventions properly. Psychological counselors—certified clinical psychologists and experienced counselors—are empathetic actors who aim to help the VEOs rejuvenate their emotions, have better ways of thinking, develop better coping strategies, build better social connections, and assist in learning pro-social behaviors in general. They can engage VEOs by creating awareness with the guidance of alternative narratives. The CTTC will form a pool of psychological counsellors and train them to deal with VEOs in and out of prison.

3.5 Religious Counsellors

Religion is a source of moral guidance and personal peace. Religious counselors can help the VEOs by providing various explanations of religious faiths to counter violent narratives. Spiritual mentorship can be a source of developing psychosocial safety and education. In the context of dealing with Islamist VEOs, religious scholars well-versed in the *Quran* (the holy book) and *Sunnah* (the life and practice of Prophet Muhammad SAW) and knowing the various schools of Islamic tradition (four Mazhabs/schools) can offer a peaceful and tolerant interpretation of Islam as an antidote to violent extremist ideas.

Religious scholars will be engaged in the planning and developing of a pedagogy for VEOs willing to accept counseling. In the implementation phase, religious counselors may be appointed by the prison authorities in consultation with the CT agencies (ATU, CTTC, and RAB). Religious counselors should share their evaluation of counseling sessions with the CT agencies and the prison authorities when needed. The evaluation reports—indicating positive or negative behavioral changes—would help redesign the religious counseling modules and practices and assess the VEOs' rehabilitation progress.

Finally, religious counsellors can inform the actors about the tolerant practices and ideas of different religious sects and clear misconceptions among themselves about the religious beliefs of the VEOs. Religious counselors may come from academic backgrounds with sufficient knowledge of subject matters.

3.6 Educational Institutions

Deradicalization programs may have two broad aims: preventing the at-risk population from being radicalized or countering the threats of radicalization through mitigating measures. In preventive aspects, educational institutions will organize awareness campaigns. In countering threats of radicalization through education, these

VEOs can gain the skills and knowledge necessary to become productive members of society and lead peaceful lives. Educational institutions (educators/subject experts) can provide various learning-based services to violent extremist offenders, including essential learning, evaluation, job-related skills, and job placement. Educators may conduct learning sessions for prison inmates to help VEOs acquire the skills and knowledge necessary after release. For out-of-the-prison former convicts, educational institutions can provide a safe and supportive environment. This can help reduce the risk of reoffending and can create a positive environment for these individuals to learn and grow. Finally, educational institutions can also provide a platform for the VEOs to share their stories and experiences. This can help reduce stigma and promote understanding between individuals with different views and beliefs. The CT agencies (ATU, CTTC, and RAB) and the Ministry of Education can select a few schools to coordinate and implement the tasks in and out of the prisons.

3.7 Vocational Skills Trainers

Vocational skills trainers from Technical and Vocational Education and Training (TVET) institutions play a pivotal role in rehabilitating violent extremist offenders. They can help these individuals develop the skills, knowledge, and attitudes necessary to reintegrate into society and lead productive and nonviolent lives. Through classroom instruction, on-the-job training, and mentoring, vocational skill trainers can help these offenders develop new employment skills and acquire the ability to ensure livelihood. Trainers can also guide and support violent extremist offenders as they transition back into the community. By providing information about local resources, such as job training, housing, and mental health services, trainers can help these individuals better understand the resources available to them and how to access them. The CT agencies of Bangladesh Police and the prison authority should partner with a few established TVET institutions to facilitate the tasks.

3.8 Cultural Organizations

Cultural organizations and activists are essential stakeholders in the deradicalization and rehabilitation of VEOs. They can help the beneficiaries better understand tolerance, cultural plurality, diversity, and peace. This understanding can lead to more effective rehabilitation efforts. Additionally, these organizations can provide resources such as mentors, cultural perspectives of society, and plural narratives and inspire the radicals for performing arts. Cultural activities provide a safe and supportive environment that can help former offenders reintegrate into society. Cultural activists can support the development of performance art networks for convicted or under-trial prisoners through lectures, workshops, and practices. This may help the suspects and the convicts develop a richer cultural perspective of life.

By providing resources such as educational materials, films, and other media, these organizations can help create a more inclusive and tolerant society. Out of the prison, cultural organizations, in collaboration with CT agencies, may organize thematic dramas, perform songs, and thus create awareness for at-risk youth communities. The ultimate goal of such cultural orientation is to promote the essence of plural nationalism, non-violence, and tolerance. Cultural actors can form support networks that can help former offenders to make positive changes in their lives and to become productive members of society.

3.9 Social Workers

Social workers can help violent extremist offenders understand the root causes of their behavior, such as childhood trauma, mental illness, and poverty. By exploring the individual's life circumstances, social workers can help the offender develop empathy and take responsibility for their actions. Through preliminary counseling, social workers can help the offender learn how to manage their emotions and use positive coping strategies, such as mindfulness and relaxation techniques, to reduce the risk of engaging in violent behavior in the future. Social workers can also provide offenders access to services, such as housing and employment support, and referrals to specialized programs, such as anger management or substance abuse treatment. These services can help the offender build the skills and confidence to reintegrate into society.

Social workers from local or national NGOs can also provide support to victims of violent extremism and their families, which can help reduce the likelihood of recidivism. Through counseling and advocacy, social workers can provide victims with the necessary resources to heal and rebuild their lives. Social workers are essential to the rehabilitation of violent extremist offenders. Their expertise, skills, and knowledge are invaluable in helping offenders understand and address the root causes of their behavior while also providing victims with the support they need to heal and rebuild their lives. Through workshops, seminars, and other forms of outreach, social workers and NGOs can help raise awareness on preventing violent extremism and the potential for rehabilitation of former VEOs. This can help reduce the stigma associated with extremism and create an environment of greater understanding and acceptance of those convicted of extremist offenses.

3.10 Business Chambers

Business chambers are vital in facilitating the rehabilitation of violent extremist offenders. Through their connections with local and regional business ventures and entrepreneurs, they can provide job training and employment opportunities for those convicted of violent extremist offenses. This is especially important, given that many former extremist offenders face immense stigma and difficulty finding gainful employment after their release from prison. Business chambers can also provide mentorship and advice to VEOs to help them adjust to life outside of prison. They can also provide access to resources such as professional development programs, job fairs, and networking events. By providing access to these resources, business chambers can help the VEOs access economic opportunities for former offenders and provide them with the support and guidance they need to reintegrate into society.

3.11 Families of VEOs and Victims

Families of violent extremists often play an essential part in their rehabilitation and reintegration into society (RAN 2018). They can help an individual adjust to everyday life. Families also offer support during recovery and can assist with figuring out how to deal with any underlying mental or emotional issues. However, they can also hinder recovery if they are not supportive or share the offender's extremist beliefs. Authorities must determine a VEO's family's level of involvement and participation in the VEO's rehabilitation process.

Victims of violent extremism and their families can also play an essential role in VEO deradicalization and rehabilitation. Support, empathy, and forgiveness from victims and their families may help violent extremists recover. This may counter the radical narrative and provide violent offenders a second chance. Victims and their families can:

- Oppose extremist beliefs by sharing their violent extremism experiences,
- Foster healing and reconciliation by promoting peace and forgiving violent extremists,
- Work with rehabilitation programs by providing practical support and resources.

It is crucial to consider and acknowledge victim families' consent and cooperation, which is critical to help rehabilitate violent extremists.

3.12 Civil Society Organizations (CSO)

CSOs can work with security agencies to design and implement deradicalization and rehabilitation programs. They can help a suspect or convict reintegrate into society by creating community awareness and maintaining liaison between the security agencies and the families. In Indonesia, CSOs have run successful community-level VEO deradicalization and rehabilitation programs in consultation with the CT agencies. They also play an essential role in getting former VEOs engaged in livelihood opportunities in their local communities. Members of the civil society in Indonesia also contribute to developing policies and programs on deradicalization. Bangladesh has a large footprint of CSOs who can meaningfully contribute to VEO deradicalization and rehabilitation.

3.13 Community Gatekeepers/Village Panchayat

Village-based community gatekeepers are local government actors and rural civil society serving as decision-making bodies and quasi-policy communities. Community gatekeepers also refer to individuals or groups within a community who have a significant influence and play a role in shaping social norms and values. The role of these includes:

- Support in alternative dispute resolution,
- Provide information regarding the progress of released VEOs,
- Implementing the process of forgiveness, understanding, and compassion,
- Supporting reintegration by helping them find jobs and education,
- Establishing bridges across communities to minimize violence and conflict, encouraging reconciliation, and
- Encouraging community-led initiatives such as community-based support groups.

Village Panchayats and community gatekeepers may foster peace, understanding, and compassion and help individuals reintegrate into society. This can help governments and other stakeholders prevent and resist violent extremism.

3.14 Political Actors

Bangladesh has a parliamentary system of democracy where both ruling and opposition parties can play a constructive role in the VEO deradicalization and rehabilitation process. The consensus among the political parties will be critical for adopting a legal and policy framework. With a sizeable grassroots support base, senior party leaders can encourage their grassroots activists to support community-based deradicalization and rehabilitation programs.

3.15 Mainstream and Social Media

Mainstream print, electronic, and social media can help deradicalize and rehab VEOs by presenting a balanced and nuanced view of the issue. They can promote alternative narratives that challenge extremist ideologies. Media can also highlight the positive efforts of governments, the private sector, and CSOs in preventing and countering violent extremism.

Newspapers can dedicate a page to sharing the experiences and perspectives of deradicalized and rehabilitated VEOs. Electronic media can also cover the life-changing stories of individuals who have walked away from the path of violent extremism. These will inspire both the at-risk population and the radicalized individuals. The media must approach the issue of violent extremism with sensitivity and avoid sensationalizing it to avoid polarizing the communities and reinforcing extremist narratives.

Social media platforms such as Facebook pages can play a unique role due to their ability to connect with many followers. They can do the following:

- Provide clear ideas about VEO deradicalization and rehabilitation programs, best practices, and success stories
- Share the stories of victims and their families to influence the hearts and minds of VEOs and their sympathizers
- Help violent extremists and their families to communicate and receive support,
- Filter violent extremist narratives and beliefs by monitoring online behaviors
- Shut down extremist websites to reduce terrorist propagation,
- Engage youth icons, religious leaders, and influencers to prevent terrorist indoctrination and counter radical ideas

3.16 Conclusion

This chapter has presented a long list of actors and stakeholders who can help an individual abandon extremist ideas and live everyday life. The remaining parts of this Handbook will provide a clear picture of more detailed roles for each actor and stakeholder. As stated in Chap. 1, these roles fall into four distinct stages: preparatory stage, deradicalization, rehabilitation, and policy reforms.

Reference

Radicalisation Awareness Network (RAN). 2018. "*RAN EX POST PAPER The Role of Family and Social Networks in the Rehabilitation of (Violent) Extremist and Terrorist Offenders.*"

Chapter 4
Capacity Building of Prison Staff and CT Professionals

4.1 Introduction

This chapter discusses the need to build the capacity of prison staff and CT professionals to manage VEO deradicalization and rehabilitation in Bangladesh. It calls for introducing the contents of knowledge and skills in countering and preventing violent extremism (C/PVE) in both basic and advanced training programs. It also stresses the involvement of various UN agencies in sharing knowledge and best practices.

4.2 Desired Outcome

Bangladesh's prison staffers and CT professionals will develop the capacity to manage prison-based and community-based programs for deradicalizing and rehabilitating VEOs.

4.3 Key Actors

Bangladesh Prisons Directorate and Bangladesh Police are the key actors responsible for managing the capacity building of prisons and CT agencies, respectively. The Prisons Directorate will run the capacity-building training for many staffers from the Prisons Directorate, the Kashimpur High-Security Prison Unit, and various central and district jails. As for the capacity building of CT agencies, the Police HQ will lead and manage the training programs in close coordination with the ATU, CTTC, and RAB. The following training facilities can be used for capacity building of prison staff and CT officials:

I. Ahmed et al., *Handbook on Deradicalization and Rehabilitation of Violent Extremist Offenders in Bangladesh*, SpringerBriefs in Environment, Security, Development and Peace 41, https://doi.org/10.1007/978-3-031-85807-9_4

- Bangladesh Prisons Headquarters, Dhaka (for approval of training contents)
- Bangladesh Jail Training Academy, Rajshahi (for imparting C/PVE in basic foundation training)
- Bangladesh Police Headquarters, Dhaka (for approval of training contents)
- Bangladesh Police Academy, Rajshahi (for imparting C/PVE in basic foundation training)
- Bangladesh Police Staff College, Dhaka (for imparting C/PVE in advanced training)

In addition, in-house training programs can be organized by the following agencies:

- Kashimpur High-Security Prisons Unit, Gazipur (for in-service training)
- Anti Terrorism Unit, Dhaka (for in-service training)
- Counter Terrorism and Transnational Crime Unit, Dhaka (for in-service training)
- Rapid Action Battalion, Dhaka (for in-service training)

Among the UN agencies, the following can be involved in the capacity building of prisons and CT professionals:

- UN Interregional Crime and Justice Research Institute (UNICRI), Turin, Italy
- UN Office on Drugs and Crime (UNICRI), Regional Office in Bangkok
- UN Asia and Far East Institute for the Prevention of Crime and the Treatment of Offenders (UNAFEI)

The involvement of the UN agencies would add value to the capacity-building programs for two reasons. First, they would transmit international best practices and act as knowledge-sharing platforms. Second, they will ensure compliance with international VEO deradicalization and rehabilitation norms.

4.4 Key Activities

(a) Conduct training sessions for prison staff.

In Bangladesh, prison staff receives basic and advanced training for managing inmates. There is a need to introduce new basic and in-service training programs on countering and preventing violent extremism (C/PVE), with specific training on managing two types of prison inmates: under-trial VEO suspects and convicted VEOs. Emphasis will be given to effective prison administration, prison intelligence, and ensuring secure custody. Prison staff also need to be aware that all prisoners shall be treated with respect due to their inherent dignity and value as human beings. Hence, the following activities are critical for the capacity building of prison staff:

- Develop a training Handbook for managing the safety and security of prison-based VEOs in Bangladesh;

- Identify the risks of prison-based radicalization and discuss these risk factors in the prison staff training
- Conduct training sessions on prisoner safety, security, radicalization risks
- Conduct training sessions on managing the deradicalization and rehabilitation of VEOs in Bangladesh.

(b) Conduct training sessions for CT professionals.

The following activities need to be carried out for the capacity building of law enforcement and intelligence practitioners involved in the deradicalization and rehabilitation of VEOs:

- Develop training Handbook on high quality and actionable intelligence gathering and analysis with an emphasis on VE threat typology (left-wing, right-wing, ethno-nationalist, and other single-issue based violent extremism); VE organizational structure (small cells, single actor, domestic group, international group, and transnational networks)
- Conduct training on Developing expertise in investigative techniques, forensic techniques, and data-sharing mechanisms.
- Conduct training sessions on risks and needs assessment of VEOs for determining the readiness of individuals considered for deradicalization and rehabilitation program
- Conduct training sessions on VEO deradicalization and rehabilitation investigation
- Exchange international best practices.

International best practices can be exchanged with countries with a longstanding tradition of managing community-based and prison-based deradicalization and rehabilitation programs (Muluk et al. 2020; NSW Department of Justice 2018; PRI 2018; Stys et al. 2016).

4.5 Methods of Operation

(a) Organize two-week-long intensive capacity-building training for Prison Staff and CT Practitioners.

The Prison Authorities, CT, and intelligence agencies will organize two-week-long intensive capacity-building training for concerned staff dealing with VEO deradicalization and rehabilitation. Two types of training modules will be included. Some modules will focus on agency-specific tasks (intelligence, operations, prison management), while others will focus on joint capacity building (inter-agency coordination).

(b) Organize a six-monthly in-service follow-up workshop.

Follow-up training sessions will be organized every six months. The goals of these follow-up training workshops are to assess the effectiveness of past training and to develop new training content.

(c) Exchange best practices

The Government of Bangladesh will organize overseas study tours for Bangladeshi prison staff, CT, and intelligence practitioners to learn firsthand international best practices in VEO deradicalization and rehabilitation. Senior C/PVE experts from UNICRI, UNAFEI, UNODC, and partner countries can also be invited to contribute to the capacity building of Bangladeshi stakeholders.

4.6 Risks and Opportunities

Risks

- Differing ideas about capacity training and capacity building needs

The prison authority and the CT and intelligence agencies may have differing ideas about the capacity-building needs for VEO deradicalization and rehabilitation. Lack of consensus on how to deal with convicted and under-trial detainees can cause such differences.

- Resource shortage

The need for more human resources in CT, intelligence, and prison agencies may reduce the opportunities for training at facilities far from the workplace. Lack of funding may also hinder capacity building at home and abroad.

Opportunities

- Currently, there is a consensus among the prison authorities and the CT agencies on starting structured programs for the rehabilitation and reintegration of VEOs. Various CT agencies have initiated pilot programs for community-based deradicalization and rehabilitation programs. They have consulted the prison authorities and developed a shared understanding for starting such programs.
- The Government of Bangladesh has also shown a willingness to commit human and financial resources to implement VEO deradicalization programs.

4.7 Monitoring and Evaluation Framework

(a) Lead Ministry

The Ministry of Home Affairs (MOHA) is the lead ministry for managing the capacity building of CT professionals and prison staff. MOHA will receive periodic reports on capacity building.

(b) Lead Agency

Bangladesh Police (ATU, CTTC, and RAB) will manage the VEO rehabilitation and reintegration programs in collaboration with various security and intelligence agencies and the Prisons Authority.

(c) Indicators

- Indicator 1: Yearly number of prison staff trained in deradicalization and rehabilitation programs
- Indicator 2: Yearly number of CT professionals trained in deradicalization and rehabilitation programs

(d) Impact Assessment

Independent evaluators will conduct a mid-term impact assessment regularly.

4.8 Conclusion

In conclusion, there is no alternative to building trained human resources and creating institutional structures for implementing this Handbook. CT professionals and prison staffers are key actors whose basic and advanced training in VEO rehabilitation will largely shape the successful outcomes in managing the threat of violent extremism.

References

Muluk, H., Umam, A. N., & Milla, M. N. (2020). Insights from a deradicalization program in Indonesian prisons: The potential benefits of psychological intervention prior to ideological discussion. *Asian Journal of Social Psychology, 23*(1), 42–53.

NSW Department of Justice. 2018. *The management of radicalized inmates in NSW.* Sydney NSW: Department of Justice.

Penal Reform International (PRI). 2015. *Summary of proceedings: Preventing radicalization in prisons: Developing a coordinated and effective approach.* Amman: PRI.

Stys, Yvonne, Rick McEachran, and Marsha Axford. 2016. *Ways Forward: Applying Lessons Learned in the Management of Radicalized Offenders to Canadian Federal Corrections.* Ottawa: Correctional Service of Canada.

Chapter 5
Screening and Admission for Assessing Readiness

5.1 Introduction

Screening and admission represent an essential step in assessing the readiness of violent extremist offenders (VEOs) for deradicalization and rehabilitation. This Chapter presents the template of Militant Activity Risks and Needs Assessment (MARNA) to be used as a screening and admission criteria for assessing the readiness of Bangladeshi militants of all ideological leanings. The proposed MARNA tool can be used to screen from a pool of VEOs willing to participate in a systematic deradicalization and rehabilitation program managed by the Government of Bangladesh.

5.2 Desired Outcome

The MARNA tool will be used to determine which of the VEOs are ready for inclusion in the deradicalization and rehabilitation program. It is desired that security and intelligence agencies responsible for managing the VEO deradicalization and rehabilitation program will use the assessment tool, continuously review its utility, and update it as needed. The tool can also be used for two other purposes. First, in the prison context, it will identify and isolate high-risk VEOs so they cannot radicalize other prison inmates and the prison staff. Second, outside the prisons, the tool can also assist in designing measures to prevent radicalization among vulnerable communities.

I. Ahmed et al., *Handbook on Deradicalization and Rehabilitation of Violent Extremist Offenders in Bangladesh*, SpringerBriefs in Environment, Security, Development and Peace 41, https://doi.org/10.1007/978-3-031-85807-9_5

5.3 Key Actors

The actors involved in the screening and admission are law enforcement and intelligence agencies, prison authorities, and forensic psychologists. CT agencies (ATU and CTTC) will primarily conduct the Risks and Needs Assessment. Designate personnel at both agencies may collaborate with the Special Branch (CT Section), National Security Intelligence (CT Wing), Directorate General of Forces Intelligence (CTIB), and competent officials of the Prisons Authority (Prisons HQ, Central Jail, or District Jail) to conduct the Risks and Needs Assessment. The CT agencies (ATU and CTTC) will engage forensic psychologists and religious scholars to carry out the Risks and Needs Assessment.

5.4 Key Activities

It is vital to note global risk assessment practices before designing Bangladesh's risks and needs assessment activities. Globally, there are four major approaches to screening through a risk assessment tool:

- Unstructured critical judgment
- The actuarial method
- Structured professional judgment (SPJ)
- A self-assessment questionnaire

The SPJ approach is more widely used and would thus be most relevant for Bangladesh. The VERA-2R (several EU countries), the ERG22+ (UK), the RRAP (EU), the IR46 (the Netherlands), the RADAR (Australia), and the RADAR-iTE (Germany) are some of the risk assessment tools that follow the SPJ model. Some of these tools aim to rehabilitate all types of VEOs (VERA-2R, ERG22+, RRAP), while others aim at Islamist militants only (IR46, RADAR, and RADAR-iTE) (UK Ministry of Justice 2019; Walkenhorst et al. 2020; AGAGD 2015).

Among Asian countries with experience in dealing with high-profile terrorist attacks, Indonesia has developed an SPJ template titled "Assessment of the Need for Development of High-Risk Criminal Category." The Indonesia Risk Assessment tool has 27 indicators clustered into five broad domains: Belief, Ideology, Social and Family Relationships, Pro-Criminal/Anti-Social Attitudes, and Attitudes toward the Republic of Indonesia. Each indicator has two possible scores: 0 for No and 1 for Yes.

The MARNA tool in Bangladesh is partly similar to the Indonesian model (for Indonesia's deradicalization, Idris, 2018; Schulze, 2008). It will be an integral part of the VEO screening and admission process. Key activities in the screening process include :

(a) Developing a Risks and Needs Assessment Tool

An essential first step in the VEO rehabilitation Handbook of Bangladesh concerns creating its own Risk Assessment Tool. The MARNA tool has 31 indicators clustered around six broad domains: Present Legal Status, Social Network, Psychological and Personality Traits, Attitudinal and Subjective Beliefs, Experiential Factors, and Criminogenic Behavior (Appendix 1). A team of researchers has jointly developed this tool at the University of Dhaka and senior with inputs from Bangladesh Police (ATU and CTTC), various intelligence agencies (DGFI, NSI, and SB), and Prisons Authority (Prisons HQ and Kashimpur High-Security Prison). The methodology for the MARNA tool development involved a review of 1,500 VEO profiles and interviews with 100 VEOs representing faith-based, ultra-left, and ethno-nationalist groups. It has also benefited from discussions with CT professionals in Indonesia and Singapore and a review of existing assessment tools in Australia, EU countries, and the UK.

(b) Piloting and Validation of the Risks and Needs Assessment Tool

The MARNA tool needs to undergo piloting and validation, which would allow it to be reviewed for necessary updating. Academic researchers with expertise in counterterrorism, security, and intelligence studies need to be involved in conducting a scientific review of the MARNA tool. Once finalized, the MARNA tool can be accepted through an official directive of the Police HQ/Ministry of Home Affairs or an official gazette notification.

(c) Training VEO Risks Assessors

CT officials, intelligence analysts, and prison staff who will be engaged in conducting the risk and needs assessment will undergo a 2-day in-house training to develop a better understanding of the MARNA indicators, the logic behind each indicator, the data sources, and the scoring system. The Assessor team will need a clear account of the VEO threat landscape, the current approaches to countering and preventing violent extremism in Bangladesh, the global trends in VE, and the utility of VEO deradicalization and rehabilitation. They also need to understand the essence of inter-agency coordination in risks and needs assessment.

(d) Choosing the Risks and Needs Assessment Sites

When an interview is conducted with the VEO, the risks and needs assessment site may vary depending on the legal status of the VEOs. Seven legal statuses can be identified: convicted and imprisoned, convicted but released after a prison term, under-trial imprisoned, under-trial on bail, indoctrinated and radicalized but not charged, self-withdrawn and not charged, and surrendered but not imprisoned. For the incarcerated VEOs (whether convicted or under trial), an interview room at the prison's premises would be ideal for conducting the risks and needs assessment. For the rest, the evaluation can be performed at the premise of a CT agency (e.g., ATU or CTT office) or a third location, whether the assessor and the VEO feel comfortable completing the process. A VEO's participation in the risks and needs assessment should be voluntary, informed, and dignified.

(e) Locating Assessment Data Sources

Data for the risks and needs assessment will come from multiple sources: an interview with the VEOs and their family members, an interview with local communities, and if possible, members of the social network to which the VEO belongs; review of case documents, including confessional statements, police reports/charge sheets, judicial verdicts; intelligence and surveillance reports; and prisons monitoring report. The interview will play an important but not the only part in the risks and needs assessment process.

(f) Conducting the Risks and Needs Assessment

The risks and needs assessment exercise shall be conducted twice a year for VEOs admitted to a deradicalization and rehabilitation program. It is necessary to monitor and evaluate whether the assessed risk level has increased or decreased for each beneficiary.

(g) Best Practice Sharing in Risks and Needs Assessment

Bangladeshi CT officials should be able to exchange their best practices with officials from bilateral development partners (Australia, UK, USA, Indonesia, Singapore) and multilateral agencies (UNODC). This would allow them to ensure that the Bangladeshi VEO risk assessment process is at par with international standards and best practices.

5.5 Methods of Operation

There are three stages in the risks and needs assessment methods of operation:

(a) Determining the Target Population

The MARNA tool focuses on various types of Bangladeshi militants, including male and female. The VEOs can come from any of the three ideological groups—faith-based, ultra-left, and ethno-nationalist. The assessment applies to VEOs maintaining any of the legal-judicial statuses mentioned above: convicted and imprisoned, convicted but released after a prison term, under-trial imprisoned, under-trial on bail indoctrinated and radicalized but not charged, self-withdrawn and not charged, and surrendered but not imprisoned.

(b) Assessment Process

The MARNA tool has five parts. The first part has 31 indicators. The assessor shall use their judgment to determine whether an indicator is present. If the answer is no, a score of zero will be given; if yes, a score of 1 will be provided. The second part of the tool requires assessing the scores and ranking them into three possible categories: High (21–31 score), Moderate (11–20 score), and Low (1–10). The assessor can record their qualitative judgment on the six broader domains in the third part. Both quantitative and qualitative judgments will be weighed to make an overall assessment.

In the fourth part, the assessor will assess the risks and recommend whether the VEO is eligible and ready for admission into the rehabilitation and reintegration program. VEOs assessed to pose low to moderate risks can be considered eligible and prepared for entry into the rehabilitation program. On the other hand, VEOs posing high risks can be screened out and deemed ineligible and not ready for participation in the rehabilitation program.

The assessor will conduct a multi-stakeholder intervention plan for the VEOs in the fifth part. Depending on the scores assigned to each of the six domains, they will receive interventions in legal counseling, psychological and religious counseling, educational and cultural orientation, and skills training.

(c) Scientific study

External Academic researchers not affiliated with the interventions should have access to the anonymized data to study the utility of the risks and needs assessment tool.

5.6 Risks and Opportunities/Mitigation Strategies

- **Risks**

  (a) The assessors may over-depend on interview and ignore other crucial pieces of information that can aid in the risks and needs assessment process
  (b) Some high-risk offenders may conceal their motivations for some of the indicators, resulting in erroneous/misleading judgment in some indicators
  (c) Bureaucratic competition among agencies (CT, intelligence, and Prisons) may impede the assessment process.

- **Opportunities**

  The following opportunities exist to mitigate the risks mentioned above:

  (a) The Research and Development (R&D) wings of CTTC and ATU have maintained an institutional repository of terrorist profiles and other documents, which can supplement the interviews and reduce over-dependence on discussions in the risks and needs assessment.
  (b) Continuous review of the assessment process can provide an opportunity to ensure the assessment is done correctly. Data triangulation will be needed to ensure the evaluation is less vulnerable to information withdrawal or concealment.
  (c) The Ministry of Home Affairs can create an inter-agency coordination mechanism to reduce bureaucratic competition among agencies involved in assessing risks and needs and implementing the VEO rehabilitation and reintegration strategy.

5.7 Monitoring and Evaluation Framework

(a) Lead Ministry

Bangladesh's lead Ministry for C/PVE is the Ministry of Home Affairs. VEO rehabilitation and reintegration are essential steps in Bangladesh's evolving C/PVE strategy.

(b) Lead Agency

Bangladesh Police, in collaboration with various security and intelligence agencies and the Prisons Authority, will manage the VEO rehabilitation and reintegration programs.

(c) Indicator

Two indicators will be used to monitor and evaluate the screening and admission process:

- Indicator 1 (on screening): The number of risks and needs assessments done every six months
- Indicator 2 (on admission): The number of VEOs enrolled in the rehabilitation and reintegration program

(a) Impact Assessment

Independent researchers should be engaged in conducting an impact assessment of the screening and admission process of VEOs. In a five-year project cycle, independent evaluators will conduct a mid-term impact assessment in the third year and an end-term impact assessment in the fifth year.

5.8 Conclusion

Risks and needs assessments are crucial for screening a large pool of target beneficiaries and determining the readiness of those who fulfill specific admission criteria for joining a VEO rehabilitation and reintegration program. The MARNA tool is developed in the Bangladesh context. Risks and needs assessors must review the tool's utility and update it periodically. CT agencies in Bangladesh shall exchange best practices with bilateral and multilateral development partners and assess the impact of the screening and admission process.

Appendix 1: Militant Activity Risks and Needs Assessment (MARNA) Tool of Bangladesh

Part I: Risk Assessment Indicators

	Yes (1)	No (0)
Domain # 1: Present Legal Status		
1. Convicted and Imprisoned	1	0
2. Convicted and released after prison term	1	0
3. Under-trial and imprisoned	1	0
4. Under-trial on bail	1	0
5. Indoctrinated but not charged	1	0
6. Withdrawn from VEO group and not charged	1	0
7. Surrendered to security forces	1	0
Domain # 2: Social Network		
1. Comes from a social group which is vulnerable to violent extremism	1	0
2. Part of a family/social network which supports violent extremism	1	0
3. Family member(s) have/has past record of involvement in violent extremist group/activities	1	0
4. The individual interviewee was once member of a violent extremist group/ discussion forum	1	0
Domain # 3: Psychological and Personality Traits		
1. Confusion about personal identity (Muslim first or Bangladeshi first)	1	0
2. Belief that individual or group identity is under threat	1	0
3. Easily manipulated by violent extremist beliefs/messages and influencers	1	0
4. Had a history of trauma or broken family issue	1	0
5. Rejected in intimate relationship	1	0
6. Possess thrill-seeking/risk-taking behavior	1	0
Domain # 4: Attitudinal and Subjective Belief		
1.1. Attracted to violent interpretation of Islam	1	0
2.2. Attracted to holy war/jihad	1	0
3.3. Attracted to the idea of ethnic insurgency/Class war	1	0
4.4. Support for martyrdom	1	0
5.5. Negative attitude toward Sufism/national integration/capitalist society	1	0
Domain # 5: Experiential Factors		
1. 1. Member of a domestic/ regional/transnational VE group	1	0
2.2. Role in a VE group (Recruiter/Financier/Intelligence Collector/Propaganda specialist/Cyber team member/Arms & Explosives handler)	1	0
3. 3. Experience of being a Foreign Fighter	1	0
4.4. Experience of longstanding deprivation	1	0

(continued)

(continued)

	Yes (1)	No (0)
Domain # 6: Criminogenic behavior		
1. 1. Past involvement in crime	1	0
2.2. Pre-radicalization involvement in crime/	1	0
3.3. Pre-radicalization conviction in a criminal offence	1	0
4.4. Involvement in a terrorist attack	1	0
5.5. Membership in a criminal organization	1	0

Part II: Assessment Score

Risk Assessment Domains	High	Moderate	Low
Domain # 1: Present Legal Status			
Domain # 2: Social Network	3–4	2	1
Domain # 3: Psychological and Personality Traits	4–6	2–3	1
Domain # 4: Attitudinal and Subjective Belief	4–5	2–3	1
Domain # 5: Experiential Factors	3–4	2	1
Domain # 6: Criminogenic behavior	4–5	2–3	1
Total			

Part III: Qualitative Assessment

Risk Assessment Domains	High	Moderate	Low
Domain # 1: Present Legal Status			
Domain # 2: Social Network			
Domain # 3: Psychological and Personality Traits			
Domain # 4: Attitudinal and Subjective Belief			
Domain # 5: Experiential Factors			
Domain # 6: Criminogenic behavior			

Note: In this part, the assessor can share any observations from the interview or documentary evidence. Such qualitative observations should supplement the quantitative assessment score.

Part IV: Overall Assessment

Assessment Criterial	Overall Judgement
Is it the first assessment?	(a) Yes (b) No

(continued)

(continued)

Assessment Criterial	Overall Judgement
Overall Assessment (What is the overall risks posed by the VEO?)	RISKS LEVEL: (a) High (21–31) (b) Moderate (11–20) (c) Low (1–10) [Note: The total score is divided by 3 to determine this risk level]
Assessor's Comment (Qualitative Judgements)	
Recommendation from External Evaluator	(a) VEO is eligible/ready for admission into the rehabilitation and reintegration program (b) VEO is not eligible/ready for admission into the rehabilitation and reintegration program

Part V: Intervention Plan

Risk Assessment Domains	Level of Risk	Type of Intervention	Frequency
Domain # 1: Present Legal Status	Low	Legal counselling	Once in 2 months
	Moderate	Legal counselling	Once a month
	High	Legal counselling	Twice a month
Domain # 2: Social Network	Low	Educational and Cultural Orientation	Once in 2 months
	Moderate	Educational and Cultural Orientation	Once a month
	High	Educational and Cultural Orientation	Twice a month
Domain # 3: Psychological and Personality Traits	Low	Psychological counselling	Once in 2 months
	Moderate	Psychological counselling	Once a month
	High	Psychological counselling	Twice a month
Domain # 4: Attitudinal and Subjective Belief	Low	Religious counselling	Once in 2 months
	Moderate	Religious counselling	Once a month
	High	Religious counselling	Twice a month
Domain # 5: Experiential Factors	Low	Skills Training	As needed
	Moderate	Skills Training	As needed
	High	Skills Training	As needed
Domain # 6: Criminogenic behavior	Low	Legal counselling	Once in 2 months
	Moderate	Legal counselling	Once a month
	High	Legal counselling	Twice a month

References

Muluk, H., Umam, A. N., & Milla, M. N. (2020). Insights from a deradicalization program in Indonesian prisons: The potential benefits of psychological intervention prior to ideological discussion. *Asian Journal of Social Psychology*, *23*(1), 42–53.

NSW Department of Justice. 2018. *The management of radicalized inmates in NSW.* Sydney NSW: Department of Justice.

Penal Reform International (PRI). 2015. *Summary of proceedings: Preventing radicalization in prisons: Developing a coordinated and effective approach.* Amman: PRI.

Stys, Yvonne, Rick McEachran, and Marsha Axford. 2016. *Ways Forward: Applying Lessons Learned in the Management of Radicalized Offenders to Canadian Federal Corrections.* Ottawa: Correctional Service of Canada.

Part II
Deradicalization

Chapter 6
Religious Counselling

6.1 Introduction

Islamist militancy as a form of faith-based extremism has emerged as a significant security threat in Bangladesh. The Holey Artisan attack of 2016 is a glaring example. This chapter analyzes how religious counseling can constitute an essential step in the deradicalization and rehabilitation of faith-based VEOs. Before designing any framework for religious faith-based counseling, it is crucial to understand how an individual turns into a faith-based extremist.

6.2 Desired Outcome

It is desired that after religious counseling, an Islamist VEO will hold a peaceful and tolerant interpretation of Islam (Boucek 2008). Religious and psychological counseling will contribute to the VEO's cognitive transformation, resulting in mental and physical disengagement from toxic ideas and extremist groups (Ahoujil 2018; Muluk et al. 2020; Altaharwah 2018; Al-Hadlaq 2015; Festinge and Carlsmith 1959).

6.3 Key Actors

- Islamic Foundation

The Islamic Foundation operates under the Ministry of Religious Affairs of the Government of Bangladesh and produces authoritative knowledge and publications on Islamic discourses. The Foundation publishes books and monographs and issues weekly Friday sermons for nationwide mosque-based Imams to follow. With support

I. Ahmed et al., *Handbook on Deradicalization and Rehabilitation of Violent Extremist Offenders in Bangladesh*, SpringerBriefs in Environment, Security, Development and Peace 41, https://doi.org/10.1007/978-3-031-85807-9_6

from academic institutions and other stakeholders, the Foundation can develop a pool of well-versed Islamic scholars who can engage in religious counseling of various VEOs, including those in prisons.

- CT Agencies of Bangladesh Police

Bangladesh's CT agencies regularly exchange ideas with mosque imams and faith groups to promote interfaith dialogues. Their role will be crucial in mainstreaming religious counseling in the country's C/PVE strategy.

- Prison Authorities

The prison authorities can engage trained religious scholars to provide counseling sessions in prison settings. Books and journals containing the peaceful narratives of Islam can be made available in prison libraries.

- Religious scholars from different schools of Islam

Religious scholars from different *mazhabs* (schools of thought) will play a role in dialogues with VEOs.

- Inter-faith dialogue leaders

Leaders from various faith groups will be essential in preaching moderation, mutual understanding, and tolerance.

- University of Dhaka

The Islamic Foundation, in collaboration with the University of Dhaka, will design and implement a digital footprint to monitor and support the state of the religious consciousness of VEOs. Islamic Foundation, in collaboration with the University of Dhaka, will offer a 3-month long training and diploma certification to the scholars who will participate in and out-of-prison counseling of the VEOs.

6.4 Key Activities

(a) Develop a communication strategy.

In collaboration with the Islamic Foundation, the CT agencies will develop a communication strategy to disseminate Islam's peaceful and tolerant messages. They will identify the toxic interpretation of *tawhid* (belief in the oneness of God), *aqidah* (creed), *manhaj* (Islamic methodology), and *jihad* (just war), and demonstrate the contexts in which certain Quranic verses were revealed and how Prophet Muhammad had championed respect for everyone including the non-Muslims and the non-believers. The CT agencies will also equip religious scholars with basic communication skills training, motivational interviewing skills, reflective listening, and questioning skills training, and logical disputing skills to engage people from every walk of life, including the VEOs.

(b) Develop a religious counseling module.

The CT agencies will develop a religious counseling module with the prison authorities and the Islamic Foundation. The module will focus on weekly individual and group sessions. They will focus on the Quranic lessons, the traditions of Prophet Muhammad, current difficulties and their creative solutions, and religious philosophies in addressing worldly challenges. Some sessions will be conducted in a group format, while others will be one-to-one.

(c) Form a Religious Rehabilitation Group

Following the Singapore model, Bangladesh can establish a Religious Rehabilitation Group (RRG) with a hotline for 24/7 communications. This will be based on the Islamic Foundation, which has a branch office in the prisons. The RRG will produce video-based lectures and handouts with alternative narratives of critical aspects of faith.

(d) Counter online extremist narratives.

RRG will work closely with the CT agencies to locate and identify extremist explanations of faith in virtual and physical spaces. It will prepare alternative explanations and dissemination plans.

(e) Digital applications

In collaboration with the Ministry of Religious Affairs and the ICT Division of The Ministry of Posts, Telecommunications, and Information Technology, the CT agencies will develop a digital application for phones and computers, which will be accessible to the beneficiaries. The mobile apps will contain interactive features with Bangla translations of the holy Quran and detailed interpretations of the most commonly used verses. It will allow the users to cross-check religious text with context and valid explanations.

(f) Modernize Imam training

The Ministry of Religious Affairs will revisit the curriculum of imams and religious clerics training. The purpose is to introduce rigorous training workshops that offer alternative narratives to counter extremist beliefs.

(g) Monitor Friday sermons and *Waz Mahfils.*

Friday sermons and *waz mahfils* (occasional religious discussions) are excellent sources of Islamic learning. The security and intelligence agencies and the Islamic Foundation need to regularly monitor the sermons and speeches delivered by the *mahfils* to see how Islam's discourses evolve and the extent to which they are vulnerable to abuse due to misinterpretation and lack of contextualization.

(h) Organize inter-faith dialogues

The Ministry of Religious Affairs, in collaboration with CT agencies, will regularly organize inter-faith dialogues to develop mutual respect and a culture of tolerance.

The government will organize international exchanges with regional scholars on religion from South and Southeast Asian countries to prevent radicalization and promote harmony and tolerance.

(i) Develop an early warning system.

Field-level NGOs and CSOs, in collaboration with the CT agencies, can develop an early warning system to detect and identify signs of faith-based extremism in a particular geographic area. Timely interventions will be needed to respond to the warning signs.

(j) Exchange best practices

Bangladeshi officials and counsellors can learn from international best practices in religious counseling and offender management. In Indonesia, prominent Islamist organizations with a mass membership base have such programs. In Singapore, a group of spiritual counselors, including mosque-based imams, preach the message of harmony, peace, and tolerance. Such best practices can prove helpful in Bangladesh.

6.5 Methods of Operations

(a) Assess faith-based knowledge

An interdisciplinary team comprising religious experts, CT professionals, and forensic psychologists will assess VEOs' current stance and vulnerability. After considering all factors, they will prepare a profile and devise an intervention strategy. This assessment will be conducted on all VEOs regardless of their legal status. The assessment process may require at least three hour-long counseling sessions.

(b) Counselling sessions on religious text and interpretation

For all types of VEOs, counseling sessions will be offered two to three times a week, depending on an intervention plan. Each session will run for 60-90 minutes. Audio-visual tools will be used during the counseling sessions. The primary goal of lessons can be initiating and accomplishing disillusionment, de-engagement from violence, then de-affiliation (de-radicalization) from the current terrorist group and current radical view, rehabilitation, and integration into society. The effort will be coordinated and progressive. Assigning religious counselors from different schools of thought or *mazhabs* will be advantageous. Religious counsellors will be trained in counter-radicalization and basic counseling.

(c) Exercise on study material

Participants in the religious counseling sessions will be assigned reading and writing exercises and can submit them when appropriate. RRG members will evaluate the training. Those who cannot write or read will have access to audio-visual study materials and voice recording devices to share their thoughts.

This exercise will be conducted on the prison premises with support from the prison staff for the prison-based convicts and under-trial detainees. For the remaining VEOs, the religious counseling sessions will be held in the RRG office, set up in the Islamic Foundation or other designated places managed by the CT agencies. The district offices of the Islamic Foundation will also host such sessions.

(d) Logistical setup in the prison cell

A specific room in prison will be used for a religious counseling program. It is important to note that the VEOs may feel resentment, develop trust issues, and be under the influence of fellow radical cellmates. The religious counselor will work closely with psychologists to build rapport, assess the mental state, and monitor progress. If necessary, s/he will motivate the VEO. Religious counselors will utilize the Handbook's tools, techniques, and expertise to facilitate ideological transformation in the VEOs. Besides, they will actively look for a potential helper from former convicted VEOs.

(e) Counseling service for the post-release VEOs

For post-release VEOs, the religious counseling support will complement the outdoor safety net support system with community gatekeepers and periodical sessions on religion, interpretations, and lifestyles. Religious leaders, including mosque-based imams, will play a proactive role in making tolerance a centerpiece of their sermons and interactions with the community. Post-release VEOs and their family members will attend counter-radicalization activities with family members.

Once the VEOs are free after their prison terms, they may be exposed to the risk of further radicalization. After release, VEOs will continue counselling sessions from RRG, the Islamic Foundation. Religious counselors and other team members will assess the risk factors and develop a safety net system to prevent relapse. This process will include the family members of POC to extend support and reduce the risk of radicalization for the VEOs and their family members. After rehabilitation and integration, the team will evaluate the POC.

6.6 Risks and Opportunities

Risks

- Some participants in the religious counseling program may hold rigid ideas and be unwilling to change their perceptions and thoughts.
- Religious counselors may have concerns over safety and security.

Opportunities

- Developing a sense of empathy among the VEOs and sharing with them the trauma of terrorist victims may prove to be effective.

- Using ex-VEOs as para-counselors will reduce costs and increase the program's creditability. They can also work as a safeguard, and the beneficiaries of religious counseling will feel effortlessly connected to them.
- A legal agreement with VEOs can minimize risk. CT agencies will provide security to the counselors, the VEOs, and their families receiving counseling.

6.7 Monitoring and Evaluation Framework

(a) Lead Ministry

The Ministry of Home Affairs, in collaboration with the Ministry of Religious Affairs (MORA), will formulate and implement religious counseling guidelines.

(b) Lead Agency

CT agencies will develop religious counseling modules in partnership with the Islamic Foundation, independent experts, academic institutions, and prison authorities.

(c) Indicators

- Indicator 1: Number of programs and varieties of programs per month and year,
- Indicator 2: Successful completion rate of the program by VEOs,
- Indicator 3: Programs designed for at-risk communities, and the number of participants and
- Indicator 4: Extremism-related offense/crime by rehabilitated VEOs.

(d) Impact Assessment

Independent evaluators will conduct a mid-term impact assessment of the religious counseling sessions.

6.8 Conclusion

The fabric of radicalization is woven into society and the community. Hence, religious counseling is critical to achieving physical and cognitive deradicalization of an individual. A multi-stakeholder counseling program will be implemented throughout the country and made an essential component of the prison management system.

References

Ahoujil, Soufiane. 2018. *Individual Presentation on The Rehabilitation and Social Reintegration of Organized Crime Members and Terrorists.* 167th United Nations Asia and Far East Institute for the Prevention of Crime and the Treatment of Offenders (UNAFEI) International Training Course Visiting Experts' Papers. Resource Material Series No. 104. Tokyo: UNAFEI.

Al-Hadlaq, Abdulrahman. 2015. "Saudi Efforts in Counter-Radicalisation and Extremist Rehabilitation." In Gunaratna, Rohan and Mohamed Bin Ali (eds.). *Terrorist rehabilitation: A new frontier in counter-terrorism.* Singapore: Imperial College Press, pp. 3-39.

Altaharwah, Ahmad N. *Rehabilitation and Social Reintegration of Organized Crime Members and Terrorists.* 167th International Training Course Visiting Experts' Papers, Resource Material Series No. 104.

Boucek, Christopher. 2008. *Saudi Arabia's "Soft" Counterterrorism Strategy: Prevention, Rehabilitation, and Aftercare.* Washington, DC: Carnegie Endowment for International Peace. Vol. 97.

Festinger, L., & Carlsmith, J. M. 1959. Cognitive consequences of forced compliance. *The journal of abnormal and social psychology, 58*(2), 203.

Muluk, H., Umam, A. N., & Milla, M. N. (2020). Insights from a deradicalization program in Indonesian prisons: The potential benefits of psychological intervention prior to ideological discussion. *Asian Journal of Social Psychology, 23*(1), 42-53.

Chapter 7
Psychological Intervention

7.1 Introduction

The extremists' radicalization process involves modifying a range of psychosocial aspects in the person, including cognitive (thoughts, beliefs), behavioral, and social processes. Thus, initiating deradicalization and disengagement from extremism requires careful consideration of the individualized assessment of the person and subsequent development and delivery of tailored psychosocial intervention for the person (Axelsson et al. 2023; Muluk et al 2020; Sukabdi 2015, 2017).

This chapter is based on narratives of several religious and leftwing extremists and some key personnel working with them. A consistent feature from these interviews was the general reflection of the extremists that they did not want to engage in those activities again, especially after going through the painful process of interrogation and detainment. Several of them were concerned about the impact of this on their family, especially their parents. Many of them mentioned that they still believe in the ideology but will not engage in faith-based or other extremist activities as they have realized this is not a suitable path at this moment/context.

The narratives collected through interviews provided more profound insights into the processes and practices involved in radicalization and violent extremism. This chapter will focus on the psychological interventions that need to be incorporated into a contextually relevant deradicalization and disengagement program for violent extremism in Bangladesh.

7.2 Desired Outcome

It is desired that an appropriate and sustained psychological intervention would facilitate cognitive reorientation of the target beneficiaries (accused, convicts, released, surrendered or suspect VEOs or at-risk population) and help them reform their

I. Ahmed et al., *Handbook on Deradicalization and Rehabilitation of Violent Extremist Offenders in Bangladesh*, SpringerBriefs in Environment, Security, Development and Peace 41, https://doi.org/10.1007/978-3-031-85807-9_7

behavior and attitudes. Cognitive reorientation will result in an individual's mental and physical disengagement from extremist ideas and affiliations.

To be more specific, the participants in the process or upon completion of the psychological intervention are expected to:

- Gain (or change to) a relatively flexible attitude and belief system aligned towards pluralism;
- accept alternative ideas, show some level of tolerant, and become increasingly distant from extremist ideas and activities;
- engage in socially acceptable alternative opportunities aligned with their life goals.

7.3 Key Actors

The government is the most robust and sustainable agency. The Ministry of Home Affairs can develop and lead a multisectoral program to coordinate and implement the strategic interventions of multiple ministries.

Critical stakeholders for successful implementation will include:

(a) Professional organizations on clinical psychology

Professional clinical psychology organizations will be key stakeholders, actively contributing by offering psychological counseling, expert opinions, and recommendations on counseling strategies. The clinical psychology department of the University of Dhaka and Bangabandhu Sheikh Mujib Medical University may be invited to collaborate with CT agencies and the prison department to lead this intervention.

(b) Security and intelligence agencies

Bangladesh's security and intelligence agencies will recruit forensic and clinical psychologists, create opportunities for them to assess the psychosocial status of VEOs, and offer them counseling and health support.

(c) Prison Authorities

The prison authorities will provide access to clinical psychologists and psycho-social counselors to conduct their services to the VEOs.

(d) Non-government developmental organizations

NGOs working on psycho-social counseling will be on board to bring the strategies to the grassroots level, implement advocacy strategies, and transform these into a social movement.

(e) Ministries/implementing agencies at the government

The Ministry of Home Affairs (MHA) and other relevant ministries will collaborate with the Bangladesh Police's CT agencies to develop policy, arrange support, connect to resources, and facilitate psychological services at the government level.

7.4 Key Activities

(a) Develop a multilevel deradicalization intervention.

The proposed intervention includes a mix of short and long-term strategies to be implemented by various stakeholders. While any organization with limited time-bound projects can implement short-term strategies, long-term interventions may require persistent efforts over decades.

Religious counseling can be crucial in initiating the journey toward deradicalization, especially for faith-based extremists. However, banking solely on spiritual counseling will not be effective in the long run, as it is amenable to changes by the same method utilized by someone with a radicalized idea. Therefore, an urgent need is to advocate for an integrated intervention infusing psychological counseling in deradicalizing and rehabilitating VEOs.

Radicalization is a complex process involving understanding perceived obligations in religion and religious practices, beliefs about eternal achievement and rewards, psychosocial crisis, worldview and thinking process, and many other aspects of an individual's life. Therefore, working with deradicalization will require multiple layers of interventions focused on specific aims addressing this process. Some will be focused on the individual level, and others on the broader community and social groups.

(b) Infuse psychological interventions into religious counseling.

Psychological counseling will be offered to reorient the meaning of religion, personal behavior, and practices. However, it will be done through a slow and careful process of assessing the existing ideas and providing access to tolerant views to the radicalized person. This is likely to cause cognitive dissonance in the person, creating an opportunity for changes in the person's existing attitudes and beliefs. The provision of materials should be aligned with the person's core values/concerns. This process of religious counseling will be based on the same method of faith and reliance on religious texts and role models. This will be more content-focused counseling, mostly self-guided but with some influence from a religious scholar in designing, accommodating, and delivering the content. The process will involve the following:

- Providing alternative ideas to think about
- Causing doubt/dissonance, preparing the ground
- Providing learning materials (book, Audio, video).

(c) Develop psychological counseling techniques.

Contrary to religious counseling, the psychological counseling component will encourage mental, especially thinking skills associated with understanding and interpreting the world and decision-making. These skills will strengthen individuals' development of logical reasoning and critical thinking. This will contribute more towards the prevention of re-indoctrination. The following activities will be practiced as counseling techniques:

- Thinking skills
- Questioning skills (Socratic questioning)
- Ability spotting/appreciative orientation
- Self-worth
- Meaning of life/goal
- Core belief (Catalyst).

(d) Enhance egalitarian values

Egalitarian values will be needed to live and interact in a pluralistic society of people from different races, religions, ethnicities, and belief systems. Implementing egalitarian values may serve as an antidote to the fixed attitude towards a single truth and may enhance the ability to empathize with people with differences. This social intervention will require well-planned and patient implementation over a long period.

- Dialogues around good citizens and good person
- Enhanced opportunities for engaging in social support activities and ensuring reinforcing consequences of such engagement.

(e) Ensuring alternative engagement

Alternative engagement may help the person sever the link with the existing circle of life and connection with radicalization. Such engagement will contribute to creating an alternative narrative for the person. Reconnecting with family relationships and responsibilities can be helpful for many, while others may need support on income generation and financial assistance programs. These alternative roles may be further strengthened by showcasing deradicalized individuals and presenting them as role models for others. The following activities will be encouraged for the VEOs:

- Involvement in family
- Income generation
- Role model and showcasing of deradicalized individuals.

(f) Exploring psychological aspects of tolerant narratives of religion

In the context of Islamist militancy in Bangladesh, radicalization involves enforcing a narrow view of Islam connected with some specific goal-directed activities. They often use examples from the sunnah to pursue their goals. Creating a tolerant narrative of Islam can be a helpful strategy. This can be done through a dual-pronged approach of directly appreciating good practices of Islam and indirectly critiquing the negative concepts (so that people will not associate those with Islam).

- Role model and showcasing of good Islam and good Muslim
- "Critiquing of negative aspects present in the narratives in Sunnah."

(g) Clarifying and Elucidating *Jihad*

Distorting the meaning of *Jihad* (holy war) is a critical feature in radicalization, especially for those involved with violent extremism. This intervention requires a combination of religious interpretation and psychological counseling through the following:

- Questioning the validity of violence in *Jihad*—whether the current form is *Jihad*, as found in the sacred texts.
- Preparation and communication of an accurate presentation of the consequences (long and short term) of Jihad to Islam and society.
- Showcasing of deradicalized individuals and their contribution to society.

7.5 Methods of Operation

The intervention will engage with the radicalized person in several phases (Fig. 7.1), namely the assessment, dissonance, psychological support, alternative identity formation, and relapse prevention phases.

(a) Assessment phase

An initial assessment of the person will be done in this phase. The person's worldview, core belief, personality pattern, and relationship will be explored, along with building

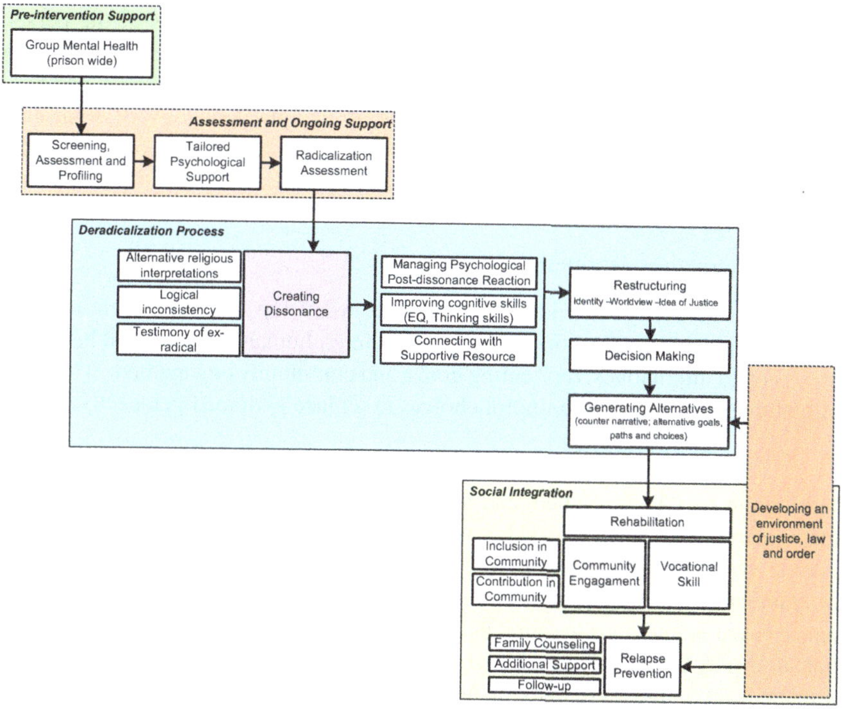

Fig. 7.1 Activities and processes in the proposed deradicalization program

necessary rapport. The assessment will contribute to creating a person's profile and identify opportunities and risks for their engagement in the intervention. Involvement in the ongoing phases will depend on the assessment data gathered in this phase. This phase will be instrumentalized in the first two months of the conviction phase of the VEOs or prison waiting-for-trial VEOs. For under-trial suspects on bail, the CT agencies will arrange counseling sessions with the help of the assigned psychologists and counselors in a neutral venue outside of the prisons.

(b) Dissonance phase

In this second phase, the person will be introduced to alternative ideas, likely to generate dissonance. The content, mode, and pace of introducing ideas will be determined based on the person's initial assessment. Correctness of the prevailing belief, authenticity, and authority of the organization and the utility and outcome of the extremist approach can be tested during this dissonance phase. Psychological counseling sessions will be designed once/twice per week, incorporating dissonance pedagogies. Two sets of sessions will be organized—in and out of prison—for convicted VEOs and on-bail accused and post-released VEOs, respectively.

(c) Psychological support phase

Based on the assessment, the person will receive psychological support in the preexisting or ongoing psychological crisis or mental health condition. Additionally, psychological support will focus on enhancing the cognitive skills of the person, which may serve to prevent reengagement from extremism. The curriculum of psychological counseling sessions will be designed to incorporate experts and practitioners from various professional segments. A sample pedagogy of counseling sessions is discussed in this document. Again, two sets of sessions will be organized—in and out of prison—for convicted VEOs and on-bail accused and post-released VEOs, respectively.

(d) The alternative identity formation phase

This phase will focus on providing opportunities to develop alternative identities. This will be done through educational components (e.g., human rights, social harmony), discussion of alternatives, reorienting goals, and community engagement. These will present the person with meaningful choices to replace extremist perspectives.

(e) Relapse prevention phase

Reinforcing social engagement and identity, engaging in income-generation activities, and providing ongoing psychological, social, and religious support will prevent relapse. The follow-up sessions on preventing relapsing to violent extremism will be significant. They incorporate counseling sessions and evaluate attendees' performance based on previous learning in the psychological counseling sessions. A set of indicators may be crucial to understanding how the experts will assess the prevention of relapse or recidivism to extremism.

7.6 Risks and Opportunities

Risks

- Lack of capacity and human resources
- The slow process of impact
- The ongoing state of injustice and socio-political turmoil
- Resistance from the extremist group
- Community acceptance of the ideologies preached by the extremists and
- The hidden nature of the activities and the problems.

Opportunities

- Political will against violent extremist
- Reduced support for extremism in the international context
- Technological advancement
- Adoption of a flexible pedagogy on psychological counseling for VEOs, which can be used to train the trainers to deal with the psychological and mental health of VEOs
- Coordinate between agencies/stakeholders to create a convenient environment for counselors to continue their interventions.

7.7 Monitoring and Evaluation Framework

(a) Lead Ministry

The Ministry of Home Affairs (MoHA) will take the lead. Other concerned ministries, including the Ministry of Health, the Ministry of Religion Affairs (MoRA), the Ministry of Youth and Sports (MoYS), the Ministry of Cultural Affairs (MOCA), and the Ministry of Women and Children Affairs (MOWCA) will provide the necessary support. The following is the planned distribution of responsibilities among the ministries:

- Overall supervision: MoHA
- Consultation: MoH, MoRA, MoCA, MoYSYouth and Sports
- Logistical Support (Space and Resource persons): MoHA, MoH, MOYS
- Gender sensitivity psychological counseling support: MOWCA.

The monitoring activities would include the following:

- Careful monitoring of the goals and objectives of the program, as well as alignment of activities with those
- Regular assessment of outcomes and impacts
- Providing feedback based on the review of ‘inputs—activities—outputs
- Keeping records of the activities being performed.

(b) Lead Agency

The CT agencies of Bangladesh Police, in collaboration with other security and intelligence agencies and the Prisons Department, will manage the psychological counseling support for VEO rehabilitation and reintegration programs.

(c) Indicators

Five indicators will be used to monitor and evaluate the psychological counseling interventions:

- Indicator 1: Yearly number of VEOs taking part in the counseling sessions,
- Indicator 2: Yearly Number of VEOs completing all counseling sessions,
- Indicator 3: Improvement in attitudes and behaviors and attitudes of participant VEOs as measured by observation reports of counselors, security professionals, and the peer group.

(d) Impact Assessment

Independent evaluators will conduct a mid-term impact assessment to study the impact of psychological counseling for VEOs.

7.8 Conclusion

This chapter provides a plan for the psychological counseling of VEOs in Bangladesh. It has been argued that cognitive disengagement of VEOs will complement other efforts to deradicalize and rehabilitate them. Careful planning, logistical support, and inter-agency coordination will be critical to successfully implementing a psychological intervention in prison or community. An interdisciplinary team must evaluate the progress toward the attitudinal and behavioral transformation of the target beneficiary.

References

Axelsson, J., Eriksson, L., & Grip, L. (2023). Managing Violent Extremist Clients in Prison and Probation Services: A Scoping Review. *Terrorism and Political Violence*, 1–24.

Muluk, H., Umam, A. N., & Milla, M. N. (2020). Insights from a deradicalization program in Indonesian prisons: The potential benefits of psychological intervention prior to ideological discussion. *Asian Journal of Social Psychology*, *23*(1), 42–53.

Sukabdi, Z. A. 2015. "A Review on Rehabilitation and Deradicalization." *Journal of Terrorism Research* 6: 35–56.

Sukabdi, Zora A. 2017. "Psychological rehabilitation for ideology-based terrorism offenders." *International Journal of Neurorehabilitation* 4 (1): 1–9.

Chapter 8
Cultural Orientation

8.1 Introduction

This Handbook defines cultural orientation as exposing the elements of national culture, heritage, and history to violent extremist offenders. The aim is to enhance their creative skills by encouraging innovative performance. The long-term goal is to develop cognitive and psycho-social transformation among the VEOs. Cultural components broadly cover national mainstream culture, inspiring the essence of Bangladesh's birth as an independent nation. It is also based on the four pillars of Bangladesh's constitution—nationalism, social justice, democracy, and secularism. The underlying assumption is that VEOs hold certain cultural beliefs. This chapter discusses the necessity of cultural re-orientation for the VEOs as a significant intervention in deradicalization and rehabilitation. It highlights the engagement of various actors who would contribute to reviving the significance of mainstream cultural knowledge among VEOs.

8.2 Desired Outcome

VEOs will have an increased understanding of mainstream culture, which will help reframe their behavioral patterns and cause them to appreciate diversity and tolerance. Moreover, improved knowledge of cultural diversity and alternative lifestyles will help VEOs understand the negative consequences of extremism (USIP 2017).

I. Ahmed et al., *Handbook on Deradicalization and Rehabilitation of Violent Extremist Offenders in Bangladesh*, SpringerBriefs in Environment, Security, Development and Peace 41, https://doi.org/10.1007/978-3-031-85807-9_8

8.3 Key Actors

(a) Ministry of Cultural Affairs

The Ministry of Cultural Affairs (MoCA) is the lead actor in Bangladesh in promoting Bangladeshi culture, heritage, and history. The Bangla Academy and the Shilpakala Academy, both of which operate under the MOCA, will play an essential role in designing the pedagogy for the cultural orientation of VEOs.

(b) Public and Private Universities

The institutes of fine arts and the departments of archeology, dance, music, and performance arts at various public and private universities will be engaged in developing tools for cultural education for both the nationwide schooling system and the prison population.

(c) CT agencies and the prison authorities

The CT agencies will bring together cultural actors into a platform to facilitate their activities of promoting cultural norms and values in society. Various types of cultural activists will be involved in developing creative skills among VEOs.

The prison authorities will also engage cultural experts as part of a larger prison-based deradicalization and rehabilitation strategy. Prison authorities can invite cultural activists who provide education and training on the local and national culture and values to VEOs. This includes teaching about the laws and regulations of the area, teaching about the local language and customs, and providing information about the history and geography of the site. The prison authorities can also support VEOs through cultural groups—drama clubs, debating groups, recitation clubs, and the like—to perform regularly and on special occasions. This can help VEOs understand the local culture and values and assist them in making positive changes in their behavior and attitudes.

(d) Cultural organizations

Several organizations in Bangladesh can work on the cultural orientation of violent extremists. These organizations include Bangla Academy, Bangladesh Shilpakala Academy, Bangladesh Udichi Shilpigoshthi, Bengal Foundation, Chhayanaut, Pathshala, and South Asian Media Institute. Their trained personnel will help VEOs understand their societies' values and norms and develop a positive attitude toward them.

(e) Civil society organizations (CSOs)

CSOs will play an essential role in providing cultural orientation to VEOs. Their programs on human rights, democratic values, gender equality, and religious tolerance will complement the works of cultural activists by highlighting the importance of positive relationships with their peers and the broader community.

(f) Sports Institutions

Sports institutions and clubs will provide a safe space for VEOs to interact with peers from different backgrounds. Bangladesh Football Federation, Bangladesh Krira Shikkha Protishtan (BKSP), Bangladesh Athletics Federation, and Bangladesh Women's Sports Federation can develop year-long and nationwide sporting competitions for the youth to develop physical strength and leadership skills. Local sports clubs will also provide mentorship programs and other support to help VEOs transition back into their communities. Since cricket and football are the two most popular sports in the country, rehabilitation efforts will benefit from engaging the VEOs in such sporting activities.

(g) TV and Radio Stations

TV and radio stations will be encouraged to develop programs that promote Bangladeshi culture and heritage. The government will sponsor short films and docu-dramas showcasing the positive role of rehabilitated individuals in promoting cultural orientation.

8.4 Key Activities

(a) Assessment of Cultural Orientation

Assessing the individual's cultural beliefs, attitudes, and motivations can provide valuable insight into why the person became involved in violent extremism (Horgan and Braddock 2010). With support from the prison authority and other security professionals, this can be done in prison for VEO inmates.

(b) Develop Contents of Cultural Orientation

CT agencies will conduct workshops with relevant cultural institutions and organizations regularly to develop the content for cultural orientation. Such contents and delivery methods will be reviewed every year.

(c) Promoting Cultural Dialogue and Practices

Providing VEOs with an opportunity to learn about the values, beliefs, and practices of their culture and other cultures can help them better understand their behavior and form a more constructive identity. This can be done by organizing in-prison cultural practice sessions on drama, debate, recitation, music, and other performance-related activities. Prison inmates can organize cultural performances in observing national days of significance. Lecture sessions on Bengali nationalism, Bangladesh's evolution, and the spirit of the 1971 War of Liberation will be organized in and out of prison for all three types of VEOs.

(d) Social Integration

In collaboration with local and national cultural and sports institutions, the CT agencies may organize various social, cultural, and sports events to help VEOs build relationships with members of other communities and foster tolerant and inclusive attitudes among them (IEP 2010).

(e) Cultural Awareness Training

Special sessions will be organized on the bridge between religious and cultural values and their compatibility in understanding the essence of life and livelihood. This can be designed for two specific and broader groups: the convicted and waiting-for-trial population and at-risk communities. The training modes will take softer approaches to explaining the significance of tolerance, diversity, religious freedom, and other national values of Bangladesh.

(f) Cultural Mentoring and Counseling

Cultural activists and educationists can support VEOs by providing one-to-one mentoring and counseling. They will collaborate with the prison authority and security sector to make positive changes in VEOs' lives and develop healthy relationships with the community.

8.5 Methods of Operations

(a) Monthly interactive discussions on Bangladeshi culture, heritage, and history

The 1971 Bangladesh Independence War and its historical background will form a basis for interactive discussions on Bangladeshi culture and heritage. Participants will be shown video content and engaged in a debate about how one should appreciate the sacrifice made by the valiant freedom fighters. Documentaries on famous archeological sites and their civilizational importance will also create a strong sense of heritage and culture. Such interactive discussions will be held monthly for all VEOs and their families.

(b) Bi-weekly training on cultural performances

The target beneficiaries of cultural orientation will meet every other week for a three-hour session to receive training on cultural performances such as drawing and painting, drama, dance, music, and recitation. Exposure to various performance art tools will enhance their cognitive and creative skills and help them find a deeper meaning in life.

(c) Sporting Competitions

The target beneficiaries will be encouraged to participate in various sporting competitions such as basketball, chess, cricket, football, and volleyball to enhance their physical fitness and develop a healthy lifestyle. Sporting celebrities will be invited to the award ceremonies.

(d) Logistical Arrangements

For prison-based VEOs (under trial or convicts), organizing monthly workshops, bi-weekly training sessions, or sporting competitions will require new logistical arrangements. The Security Service Division of the Ministry of Home Affairs will allocate necessary resources to ensure the logistical arrangements meet the requirements of the cultural orientation of deradicalization and rehabilitation programs. The CT agencies will develop a pool of cultural experts and sports trainers who will visit the prisons and organize various sessions in the presence of correctional officers and other relevant prison officials.

For other beneficiary groups, including the post-release VEOs, under-trial VEOs on bail, surrendered VEOs living freely, and at-risk populations, the CT agencies will develop regional programs to cater to the needs of people from various geographic areas. Resource persons will come from cultural organizations, university-based institutes and departments, and sporting clubs. Local NGOs and CSOs will be essential in such activities in remote places.

8.6 Risks and Opportunities/Mitigation Strategies

Risks

- The risk of cultural orientation for VEOs lies in the potential for the offenders to interpret cultural values and norms in ways that could support or further their violent extremist beliefs (CREST 2021). This could lead to furthering the extremist ideology and possibly even recruiting new members.
- Some cultural narratives may be misinterpreted as alien and not consistent with the religious values of some participants.
- It is also possible that the cultural orientation might cause the VEOs to become more entrenched in their beliefs, decreasing their likelihood of rehabilitation.

Opportunities

- The opportunity lies in the potential for cultural orientation to provide VEOs with a more accurate and nuanced understanding of cultural values and norms.
- Cultural and sporting events will create a bridging point for cultural and religious beliefs
- If delivered with caution and sensitivity by qualified professionals, cultural orientation will produce a better outcome in deradicalization and rehabilitation.

8.7 Monitoring and Evaluation Framework

(a) Lead Ministry

As the lead Ministry for implementing VEO deradicalization and rehabilitation, the Ministry of Home Affairs will partner with the Ministry of Cultural Affairs, the Ministry of Youth & Sports (MOYS), and the Ministry of Women and Children Affairs to develop and implement tools and techniques of cultural orientation.

(b) Lead Agency

The CT agencies will coordinate the delivery of cultural and sporting interventions in various settings. They will partner with the concerned prison authorities to run activities for prison-based cultural orientation.

(c) Indicators

- Indicator 1 (Planned activities): Number of cultural orientation sessions (monthly workshops, bi-weekly training sessions, or sporting competitions) planned every year
- Indicator 1 (Delivered activities): Number of cultural orientation sessions (monthly workshops, bi-weekly training sessions, or sporting competitions) organized every year

(d) Impact Assessment

Independent evaluators will conduct a periodic assessment to show results of what worked and what did not among the various tools of cultural orientation.

8.8 Conclusion

VEOs will receive consultations on the concepts and practices of cultural awareness through training and workshop sessions in and outside the prison. They will be oriented with a comprehensive understanding of national/mainstream culture through its various forms—music, plays, literature, debates, recitation, etc. This will refresh their minds and body and encourage their creative skills.

The VEOs are expected to improve their communication skills. This orientation will also positively affect religious practices, helping foster a more respectful and inclusive society.

References

Centre for Research and Evidence on Security Threats. 2021. *A guide to deradicalisation and disengagement programming*. CREST Research.

Horgan, J., and Braddock, K. 2010. Rehabilitating the terrorists?: Challenges in assessing the effectiveness of deradicalization programs. *Terrorism and Political Violence* 22 (2): 267–291.

Institute for Economics & Peace. 2010. *Beyond terrorism: Deradicalization and disengagement from violent extremism*. International Peace Institute.

United States Institute of Peace. 2017. *Deradicalizing, rehabilitating, and reintegrating violent extremists: Lessons from the global community*. United States Institute of Peace.

Chapter 9
Social Harmony, Pluralism, and Tolerance Through Education

9.1 Introduction

Social harmony, pluralism, and tolerance are essential values that can promote peaceful coexistence in diverse societies. However, VEOs often adopt beliefs and behaviors that challenge these values, which lead to social cleavages and acts of terrorism. Bangladesh's most standard social factor behind intolerance is a decline in the knowledge of harmony and diversity, including scholarship on religions, ethnicities, and pluralism. In Bangladesh, the existing socioeconomic, cultural, religious, structural, and interpersonal dynamics trigger intolerance and extremism among the various groups, both empowered and disempowered, who are susceptible to radicalization and extremism. The interpersonal factors can be depression, deprivation, cut-throat competition, and personal trauma, including bullying, childhood abuse, and family death. The structural factors specific to South Asia, including Bangladesh, can be the shrinkage of liberal space and critical thinking, deficiencies in the education systems, and the experience of discrimination (Ahmed 2006, 2009, 2014, 2020, 2021).

Tolerance education can play a crucial role in countering intolerance and violent extremism by promoting social harmony, pluralism, and tolerance. By providing the VEOs with a comprehensive and nuanced understanding of different cultures, religions, and perspectives, education can help them develop empathy and respect for others (Jugl 2022). Moreover, education can equip VEOs with critical thinking and problem-solving skills, enabling them to challenge violent extremist ideologies and find non-violent solutions to conflicts. Overall, education through social harmony, pluralism, and tolerance for VEOs can contribute to creating more inclusive and peaceful societies.

I. Ahmed et al., *Handbook on Deradicalization and Rehabilitation of Violent Extremist Offenders in Bangladesh*, SpringerBriefs in Environment, Security, Development and Peace 41, https://doi.org/10.1007/978-3-031-85807-9_9

9.2 Desired Outcome

The desired outcome of promoting social harmony, pluralism, and tolerance through education is to increase empathy and mutual understanding in society. It will also reduce violence and radicalization into violent extremism through improved community relations. The diversity in the social fabric will be highlighted, leading to effective rehabilitation and reintegration of VEOs.

9.3 Key Actors

- The Ministry of Education and the Ministry of Cultural Affairs will play a key role in implementing educational programs on cultural diversity, social harmony, and tolerance, targeting a broad stratum of society.
- The counterterrorism (CT) agencies (ATU, CTTC, and RAB) will impart tolerance education as part of their VEO deradicalization and rehabilitation programs.
- The prison authorities will include diversity and tolerance education for the imprisoned VEOs.
- Educators from the primary, secondary, and tertiary level institutions will be engaged in developing curricula and delivering lessons on various issues related to social harmony, pluralism, and tolerance.
- Civil Society Organizations (CSOs) with extensive field-level experience will share their knowledge and expertise on best practices in social harmony in Bangladesh.

9.4 Key Activities

(a) Need Assessment

In collaboration with the prison authorities, the CT agencies will conduct a need assessment of education on pluralism, tolerance, and social harmony. The need assessment exercise will determine the relevance and use of various components in conducting education sessions for targeted beneficiary groups.

(b) Curriculum Development

The course contents may include theories and practices of tolerance, the civilizational quest, and the linkage between tolerance, justice, and globalization. It will also discuss festivals and foods, communal harmony, inter-religious dialogues, and Bangladesh's heritage.

(c) Training of the Trainers (ToT)

A multidisciplinary group of educators will be trained to disseminate knowledge of harmony, inclusion, and tolerance. Based on their experience and exposure to the relevant training capacities, the educators will be drawn from various academic institutions.

(d) Program Delivery

Tolerance education should include religious and psychological counseling, cultural orientation, and legal counseling. The lessons can be offered in a daylong classroom setting, a virtual platform, and through residential workshops.

(e) Developing a Bangladesh Center for Tolerance and Diversity

A Bangladesh Center for Tolerance and Diversity (BCTD) will be established, offering tolerance education throughout the year. The BCTD will manage data on VE trends, run youth and community engagement programs, and make tolerance lessons part of mainstream education.

9.5 Methods of Operation

(a) Develop a multi-level comprehensive program.

A comprehensive program will be developed with multiple counseling sessions on educating tolerance, pluralism, and social harmony. The session topics will consider the following modalities.

Collaborative approach: Collaboration between the abovementioned actors in identifying the issues and modes of education.

Culturally sensitive approach: The topics must be culturally sensitive and inclusive of cultural diversity.

Evidence-based approach: The discussions will focus on evidence from existing studies on preventing and countering violent extremism through harmony and diversity. The South Asian regional and international best practices will be thoroughly discussed. Bangladesh's long tradition of social peace and tolerance will also be addressed.

(b) Interactive teaching methods

Each session will follow an interactive and participatory approach. The counselors will use positive and different examples. Various tools that may inspire the VEOs' creative and critical thinking will be utilized to facilitate the concepts of plurality and social harmony.

(c) Use of technology

Counseling sessions will use multimedia projectors, sound systems, electronic boards, high-speed internet, and other appropriate technologies. These instructional technologies will enable counselors to use short video documentary movies, audio-visual content, and online education materials.

(d) Flexibility and adaptability

Training techniques will be flexible. They will adopt new ideas and tools that have evolved from evaluating the interventions. Based on the feedback from educators, CT, and prison staff, new ideas and topics will be incorporated into this process.

9.6 Risks and Opportunities/Mitigation Strategies

Risks

- Some participants may express an explicit interest in attending tolerance education programs while implicitly denying their relevance.
- Tolerance education is an expensive proposition. Funding shortages may undercut the efficacy of such programs.
- Some of the participants may confront social stigma if they are branded as violent extremists.
- If tolerance education is separate from a long-term and life-long educational program, it may have limited Impact.

Opportunities

- Families and local communities can be involved in the tolerance education project to ensure that released convicted VEOs, under-trial detainees, and at-risk populations are committed to social harmony, pluralism, and tolerance.
- Public-private partnerships and development partner's support can mitigate the risk of a funding shortage.
- Community involvement is critical to overcoming social stigma.
- Educational institutions can be engaged in integrating the spirits of social harmony and diversity to build an inclusive and tolerant society.

9.7 Monitoring and Framework

(a) Lead Ministry

The Ministry of Home Affairs, in collaboration with the Ministry of Education and the Ministry of Cultural Affairs, will formulate and implement tolerance education programs.

(b) Lead Agency

CT agencies will partner with the prison authorities and a multi-disciplinary group of tolerance educators to run the community-based and prison-based tolerance education program.

(c) Indicators

- Indicator 1: Number of programs and varieties of programs per month and year,
- Indicator 2: Successful completion rate of the program by VEOs,
- Indicator 3: Extremism-related offense/crime committed by the participants of the tolerance education program.

(d) Impact Assessment

Independent evaluators will assess the educational sessions' impact to promote social harmony, pluralism, and tolerance.

9.8 Conclusions

Promoting social harmony, pluralism, and tolerance through education for VEOs is crucial for deradicalizing violent extremist offenders and preparing them for rehabilitation and reintegration into society. Developing appropriate curricula and pedagogy and continuously assessing such educational programs is essential for Bangladesh's peaceful and inclusive culture.

References

Ahmed, Imtiaz, ed., 2006. *Understanding Terrorism in South Asia: Beyond Statist Discourses* Colombo: Regional Centre for Strategic Studies and New Delhi: Manohar Publishers.

Ahmed, Imtiaz, ed., 2009. *Terrorism in the 21 st Century: Perspectives from Bangladesh.* Dhaka: University Press Limited.

Ahmed, Imtiaz, ed., 2014. *Human Rights in Bangladesh: Past, Present & Futures*, Dhaka: University Press Limited.

Ahmed, Imtiaz. 2020. *Civil Society, State & Democratic Futures in Bangladesh*, Dhaka: Prothoma Prokashan.

Ahmed, Imtiaz. 2021. *Extremist narratives for political gains: Bangladesh, India, and Sri Lanka.* CGS Paper 10, Centre for Genocide Studies, University of Dhaka, October 2021.

Jugl, I. 2022. Breaking up the Bubble: Improving critical thinking skills and tolerance of ambiguity in deradicalization mentoring. *Journal for Deradicalization*, (30), 45–80.

Chapter 10
Legal Counselling

10.1 Introduction

The Anti Terrorism Act 2009 and other relevant laws constitute a salient feature of Bangladesh's evolving criminal justice system. This chapter discusses how knowledge of these laws can contribute to deradicalization and rehabilitation efforts. Legal counseling creates legal awareness for preventing crimes and building a resilient society. Counselors can help beneficiaries by exchanging their experiences non-intrusively and explaining the legal support and protections available to those who cooperate. In addition, legal counseling can assist by providing details on resources/ information that can be used to prevent violent extremism.

10.2 Desired Outcome of Legal Counselling of VEOs

Legal counseling will enhance the participants' respect for the rule of law and prevent them from supporting or committing extremist offenses.

10.3 Key Actors

(a) CT professionals

CT professionals are the first line of defense in the fight against violent extremism. They want people to abide by laws and avoid criminal and extremist activities.

(b) Legal Aid service providers

Several civil society organizations, such as the Ain O Shalish Kendra (ASK), Bangladesh Legal Aid Service Trust (BLAST), and Bangladesh National Women

I. Ahmed et al., *Handbook on Deradicalization and Rehabilitation of Violent Extremist Offenders in Bangladesh*, SpringerBriefs in Environment, Security, Development and Peace 41, https://doi.org/10.1007/978-3-031-85807-9_10

Lawyers' Association (BNWLA), provide free legal counseling to low-income people. The knowledge and expertise of these legal aid service providers will be used to offer legal counseling throughout the country.

(c) Judiciary

The Anti-Terrorism Tribunals and the Office of the Attorney General will ensure that legal counseling services are accessible to under-trial detainees on bail and in prisons. Public prosecutors of the Anti-Terrorism Tribunals will also be recruited to maintain the highest level of transparency in the counseling programs.

10.4 Key Activities

(a) Developing a Handbook for legal counseling

A multi-disciplinary team of legal experts and CT professionals will develop a module for legal counseling. The module will feature the following laws:

- Anti Terrorism Act 2009 (including amendments)
- Money Laundering Prevention Act 2012
- Anti Terrorism Rules 2013
- Explosives Act 1884
- Explosive Substances Act 1908
- Arms Act 1878
- Special Powers Act 1974
- Penal Code 1860
- Digital Security Act 2018
- Anti Terrorism Unit Rules 2019.

The team will decide which provisions of these laws are to be included in the counseling module. Provisions related to the definition of terrorism, terrorist acts, radicalization, radicalization process, terrorist financing, use of digital media for terrorist offenses, and punishment for various crimes related to involvement in a violent extremist group or supporting such groups will be detailed (read UNICRI and GCTF, 2019, for a better understanding of the crime-terror nexus).

(b) Training legal counselors

A group of legal counsellors will be trained to ensure they understand the ultimate goal of legal counseling, which is the deradicalization and rehabilitation of VEOs in Bangladesh. The counselors will be trained to develop compassion, empathy, and the skills to win beneficiaries' trust.

(c) Exchange international best practices

The CT agencies in Bangladesh will exchange international best practices to learn about what works best and what does not in the context of legal counseling for deradicalization and rehabilitation (UK Home Office 2015, 2018, 2019; UNICRI 2016).

(d) Develop an assessment tool to observe improvement in knowledge of C/PVE laws

After a series of legal counseling sessions, the CT agencies will assess whether the counseling enhanced the participants' knowledge of laws concerning countering and preventing violent extremism (C/PVE) in Bangladesh.

10.5 Methods of Operation

(a) Develop a policy framework for counseling

The Ministry of Home Affairs, in collaboration with the Police Headquarters, will develop a policy for offering counseling services. The policy framework will spell out the educational and professional backgrounds of the counsellors. They will have a minimum bachelor of law degree with at least three years of counseling services.

(b) Counselling centers

Participants in the counseling sessions will include the following categories of individuals:

- under-trial VEOs on bail
- under-trial VEOs in prisons
- surrendered VEOs
- at-risk population
- post-release VEOs.

The prisons will arrange a room for the legal counseling of under-trial VEOs. Those with lower crimes will be the ideal candidates for counseling, as they will be advised to refrain from committing crimes to avoid stringent punishment.

For the rest, the counseling centers will include law schools or designated places to offer other types of counseling, including religious and psychosocial therapies.

(c) Audiovisual learning tools

The legal counseling sessions will be interactive and use audiovisual learning tools. The discussions will use real-world cases in which participants will see the traumatic effects of violent extremism on the lives of victims and their families and the legal consequences of involving in violent extremism.

(d) Session plans

Depending on the vulnerability to extremism and the level of involvement in violent extremism, each prison-based VEO and under-trial detainee on bail will receive six individualized counseling sessions over six months. Each session will run for

90 min. An assessment will be conducted after the completion of six sessions. Group sessions will be conducted for the remaining VEOs (at-risk population, surrendered VEOs, and post-release VEOs). CT agencies will organize two-day workshops on various campuses of educational institutions to create awareness among the young population attending schools, colleges, universities, and *madrasahs*.

10.6 Risks and Opportunities/Mitigation Strategies

Risks

- Some VEOs in the prisons may not be willing to cooperate and speak frankly during the legal counseling sessions
- Some counselors may be concerned about their safety and security
- shortage of skilled and well-informed legal counselors (in the prisons and community settings) may hinder the counseling plans.

Opportunities

- Legal counseling will start with those willing to attend such sessions voluntarily.
- Participants will be offered a wide variety of incentives. For instance, prison-based VEOs may be offered better cells and more family visits to secure cooperation.
- Plainclothes security will be provided to counselors.
- Intensive programs are currently underway to train lawyers in the emerging body of laws related to C/PVE.

10.7 M&E Framework

(a) Lead Ministry

The Ministry of Home Affairs is the lead Ministry for organizing legal counseling for the deradicalization and rehabilitation of VEOs. The Ministry of Law, Justice, and Parliamentary Affairs will co-lead legal counseling on C/PVE purposes.

(b) Lead Agency

The CT and prison authorities are the lead agencies for managing legal counseling. Legal aid services provided by CSOs will support them.

(c) Indicators
- Number of legal counseling sessions planned
- Number of legal counseling sessions offered.

(d) Impact Assessment

Independent researchers should have access to data to evaluate the impact of the legal counseling service in both prison and non-prison/community settings.

10.8 Conclusions

Legal counseling provides a trustworthy environment for the beneficiaries to learn about their duties and rights as responsible citizens. The counseling sessions will provide the necessary information and guidance to the beneficiaries regarding the legal factors of countering and preventing violent extremism. It can also help the beneficiaries learn various aspects of CT operations, particularly the legal basis of such operations. Bangladesh has a robust legal system for dealing with the threat of violent extremism. The comprehensive legal counseling system offered in this Handbook will have a long-term effect in deradicalizing and rehabilitating individuals with violent extremist beliefs.

References

UK Home Office. 2015. *Channel Duty Guidance: Protecting vulnerable people from being drawn into terrorism*. London: Home Office.

UK Home Office. 2018. *The United Kingdom's Strategy for Countering Terrorism*. London: Home Office.

UK Home Office. 2019. *Individuals referred to and supported through the Prevent program*. London: Home Office.

United Nations Interregional Crime and Justice Research Institute (UNICRI). 2016. *Children and Counterterrorism*. Turin: UNICRI.

United Nations Interregional Crime and Justice Research Institute (UNICRI) and Global Counterterrorism Forum (GCF). 2019. *Policy Toolkit on the Hague Good Practices on the Nexus between Transnational Organized Crime and Terrorism*. Turin: UNICRI.

Part III
Rehabilitation

Chapter 11
Physical Disengagement

11.1 Introduction

Disengagement is a behavioral change where individuals cease involvement in violent extremist groups and activities. It entails a shift in one's behavior away from violence. Disengagement is distinct from the attitudinal deradicalization process, in which individuals abandon their belief in a violent, extremist ideology. Importantly, disengagement and deradicalization often do not coincide. Individuals may disengage from violent extremism without relinquishing their faith in the violent extremist ideology (Gunaratna 2015; ICCT 2012; ICPTR 2010).

Moreover, not all individuals participating in violent extremism are driven by a deep commitment to the doctrine or cause. Some are not "radicalized" but forced to join or motivated, for example, by the opportunistic gains of involvement (e.g., salary, looting), a desire to engage in violence of any kind, etc. Likewise, many individuals believe in violent extremist ideologies and are not involved in violent extremist or illegal behavior.

11.2 Desired Outcome

It is desired that individuals participating in the deradicalization and rehabilitation programs in Bangladesh will not only abandon their extremist beliefs but also physically disengage themselves from participating in any violent extremist activities such as recruitment, propaganda, training, funding, and operations.

I. Ahmed et al., *Handbook on Deradicalization and Rehabilitation of Violent Extremist Offenders in Bangladesh*, SpringerBriefs in Environment, Security, Development and Peace 41, https://doi.org/10.1007/978-3-031-85807-9_11

11.3 Key Actors

Some crucial actors that can work as the catalyst in behavioral change for physical disengagement are listed below.

(a) Prison authority

A militant, terrorist, or VE is usually in jail during the trial process (one might also get bail based on the gravity of the crime) or after conviction. During this time, the prison authority will constantly monitor the VEOs, which is why the prison authority can play a vital role in achieving physical disengagement.

(b) Law enforcement agencies

The police, as the leading law enforcement authority in Bangladesh, is engaged with terrorists or VEs from the identification process of the accused to the verdict and even afterward. As a result, in Bangladesh, the police will always play a key role in achieving physical disengagement.

(c) Friends and family

Whether a person is accused or acquitted of violent extremism charges, friends and family will always impact their decision-making process. As a result, they are one of the crucial factors in ensuring physical disengagement.

(d) Religious leaders and institutions

One of the most exploited ways to radicalize a person is by misinterpreting the Holy Scriptures (in this case, the Holy Quran). Religious leaders and institutions are vital in countering such radicalization and physical disengagement by spreading the true essence of Islam.

(e) Professional counselors and Psychiatrists

Before starting the physical disengagement process, one must understand the mental state of the radicalized person, and psychiatrists can play a crucial role. Based on the findings of the psychiatrists, the counselors can make plans for counseling sessions, and proper authorities can monitor the progress.

(f) Social workers

VE convicts are expected to reintegrate into society after their time in prison. During the reintegration process, one of the significant issues that one faces is the availability of livelihood for such persons, as the general masses have a sense of skepticism regarding them. Also, in many cases, such persons lack job skills and sometimes turn back to terrorism or extremism from frustration. To avoid such a scenario, social workers can play a vital role. Social workers might meet and communicate with such prisoners six months or one year before the end of the imprisonment time, analyze the person's ability, and make livelihood training recommendations accordingly.

(g) Deradicalization centers

The concept of deradicalization centers is still in its early stages of development in Bangladesh, but they can play a crucial role in disengagement. Deradicalization centers also work as a medium of reintegration into society; as a result, they are critical actors.

11.4 Key Activities

(a) Motivation, mental support, and counseling

A complete physical disengagement will require a person to let go of the ideological belief of the terrorist group and restrain oneself from acting violently to establish their trust. To achieve this, a person must undergo a process that requires mental strength and motivation. To accomplish this, a person requires mental support and counseling from the key actors. In the initial stage, certified forensic psychologists will be needed to assess the radicalized person's mental state. Based on that, a counseling and medication plan can be prepared on how to proceed, and this procedure might vary from subject to subject. The plan must include the other key actors to reach the physical disengagement state.

(b) Training and reintegration into society

Reintegration into society is the most challenging part of ensuring physical disengagement. Providing training is a good solution in this regard. In this context, training is of two types. Firstly, training for reintegration into society might include behaving with the general mass, responding if someone talks about the past, and acting calmly even in a difficult situation. The second type of training is required for livelihood. In most cases, the convicted VEOs must have the necessary livelihood skill sets. They need to be trained on such skills during their imprisonment tenure and utilize them to build a better life once they are out of jail.

(c) Monitoring

The monitoring should start once a person is accused of terrorist or VE activities (whether s/he is on bail or in jail). If the person is on bail, the specialized police unit (such as ATU or CTTC) needs to keep such persons under watch. If the person is in jail, it is the responsibility of the prison authority to make sure that the person goes through the process of disengagement.

11.5 Methods of Operation

(a) For Under Trial (On Bail and In-Prison) Detainees

Suppose an accused person (VE cases) is on bail. In that case, they will be provided counseling services under the deradicalization centers run by ATU, CTTC, RAB, or other CT agencies. He will also need to be under the monitoring of law enforcement agencies. The agencies will communicate with them from time to time to learn about their whereabouts and livelihoods.

In cases where a person is under trial but in jail, it will be required to provide him with both counseling and training services. Even if a person is in prison, relevant law enforcement agencies like (ATU or CTTC) need access to jail for monitoring and communication purposes in addition to the surveillance of the prison authority.

(b) For Convicted Detainees

It is crucial to provide counseling services to convicted detainees from the beginning of the detention period (for further reading on Sri Lanka's experience, read ICJ 2010; Sri Lanka Ministry 2009).

One year before the end of the imprisonment period, the prisoner should be provided with training on reintegration and livelihood, and the proper actors should be consulted.

Suppose a person is imprisoned for less than a year; in that case, the counseling and training program should start immediately so that by the time the person returns to society, s/he will be fully ready to cope and integrate with it. Even in these scenarios, relevant law enforcement authorities (ATU or CTTC) must have access to the jail for monitoring purposes.

(c) For Post-Release VEOs

In this case, the post-release VEOs are expected to have received the necessary training and counseling during their time in jail. The only important thing that is required is continuous monitoring. The approved deradicalization centers should play the central role here. The deradicalization centers must communicate with local social welfare workers to find suitable jobs for such persons according to their qualifications (if required). The deradicalization centers will also be responsible for keeping track of the VEOs' whereabouts. It should also arrange for psychiatrists to test the post-release VEOs' mental state annually and take necessary actions accordingly.

11.6 Risk and Opportunities

Risks

(a) It has been found that some of the VEOs return to their previous state, especially during the bail period. This is one of the areas when monitoring is crucial.
(b) It has also been observed that in some cases, the detained VEOs conduct group meetings within the jail premises and sometimes even plan for sabotage. Prison authorities need to ensure that no such meeting occurs within the prison.
(c) Another observation is that juvenile offenders might become hardened VEOs by mixing with the old masterminds in jail. Here, the jail authority needs to play an active role in ensuring no such thing happens.

Opportunities

The law enforcement authorities will be willing to collaborate on such programs as they would provide the opportunity to reduce terrorist threats within the country. Law enforcement authorities should be allowed to work and collect information from prisons to achieve that. The Prisons Authority needs to ensure that the monitoring of the prison remains top-notch.

11.7 Monitoring and Evaluation Framework

(a) Lead Ministry

The Ministry of Home Affairs (MOHA) will ensure that deradicalized and rehabilitated VEOs do not engage in extremist groups and activities.

(b) Lead Agency

Among the CT agencies, the ATU, CTTC, and RAB may run deradicalization centers for cognitive and physical disengagement of VEOs. Designated personnel at the CT agencies will report on the whereabouts and livelihood issues of the VEOs every three months. The deradicalization centers will also send a psychological report on the VEOs annually to law enforcement agencies. The Prisons Authority will ensure that prison staff takes appropriate steps to deny the imprisoned VEOs (whether under trial or convicted) any opportunities for engaging in VE activities.

Law enforcement authorities should have databases to keep records. These records will only be accessible by designated officers, and a log history must be kept for audit purposes. These data centers should have a link to Bangladesh Police Headquarters. Only certain designated persons from the headquarters should have access to these databases, but they should not be provided access to rewrite data. They will only have read-only access.

A central committee should be formed at the Police headquarters to monitor these initiatives. The committee should meet every six months to assess progress and provide policy guidelines.

(c) Indicator

The following indicators can be used for physical disengagement purposes:

- Indicator 1 (Social engagement): The number of social activities the VEOs have participated in yearly.
- Indicator 2 (C/PVE engagement): Yearly number of activities related to countering and preventing violent extremism (C/PVE) that the VEOs have participated in.

(d) Impact Assessment

Independent evaluators will conduct mid-term and end-term impact assessments.

11.8 Conclusion

This chapter has described the overall process of disengagement for the VEOs to return to everyday life and be accepted by society. There is the risk of the VEOs returning to their old beliefs, which must be mitigated with joint tasks from the stakeholders. CT agencies must collaborate closely with the prison authority and the deradicalization centers to monitor and train the VEOs. The MOHA, the ministerial lead, must ensure coordination among the ministries. Still, at the field level, the CT agencies must take the lead in monitoring and disengagement.

References

Gunaratna, Rohan. 2015. "Terrorist Rehabilitation: Genesis, Genealogy and Likely Future." In Gunaratna, Rohan and Mohamed Bin Ali (eds.). *Terrorist rehabilitation: A new frontier in counter-terrorism*. Singapore: Imperial College Press, pp. 41–70.

International Centre for Counter-Terrorism (ICCT). 2012. *Roundtable Expert Meeting & Conference on Rehabilitation and Reintegration of Violent Extremist Offenders: Core Principles & Good Practices*. ICCT Background Paper. The Hague: ICCT.

International Commission of Jurists (ICJ). 2010. *Beyond Lawful Constraints: Sri Lanka's Mass Detention of LTTE Suspects*. ICJ Briefing Note. Geneva: ICJ.

International Centre for Political Violence and Terrorism Research (ICPTR). 2010. *1st Strategic Workshop on Rehabilitation and De-Radicalization of Militants and Extremists*. Singapore: ICPVTR.

Sri Lanka Ministry of Disaster Management and Human Rights. 2009. National Action Plan of the National Framework Proposal for Reintegration of Ex-combatants into Civilian Life in Sri Lanka. Colombo: Ministry of Disaster Management and Human Rights.

Chapter 12
Academic Training

12.1 Introduction

This chapter discusses the role of academic training as a core component in the rehabilitation process of violent extremist offenders (VEOs). VEOs, whether living in the community or housed in prisons, must have access to formal education and skills training opportunities (Koehler and Fiebig 2019). This will enhance their employability and chances of remaining engaged in productive income-generating activities, which are crucial for rehabilitation and reintegration into society.

This Handbook assumes that academic training can help tackle the underlying causes of violent extremism, empower people, and strengthen communities. Participants will study basic subjects based on their levels of schooling. In addition, emphasis will be given to critical thinking, problem-solving, reading, writing, and mathematics. Educators can boost participants' knowledge-seeking endeavors and ensure the recognition of formal education, either in prison or post-prison, thus promoting their chances for employment and entrepreneurship. Educational programs can help individuals regain their self-esteem and purpose in life (Khalil, Zuethen and Marsden 2023).

12.2 Desired Outcome

Convicted or suspected VEOs who do not have formal education or could not finish their formal education should have opportunities to continue their studies and attend skills training programs. Formal education and skills training programs will pave the way for the VEOs to rehabilitate and reintegrate into society.

I. Ahmed et al., *Handbook on Deradicalization and Rehabilitation of Violent Extremist Offenders in Bangladesh*, SpringerBriefs in Environment, Security, Development and Peace 41, https://doi.org/10.1007/978-3-031-85807-9_12

12.3 Key Actors

(a) Ministry of Education

The Ministry of Education should develop policies for extending educational opportunities to students who drop out of schools, colleges, universities, or madrassahs for various reasons, including radicalization into violent extremism. The Ministry should also adopt policies for continued educational opportunities for prison inmates. Such options must be available in Bangladesh and many countries like Singapore.

(b) Primary and Secondary Education Boards

The primary and secondary education boards in Bangladesh oversee elementary and secondary education curriculum, evaluation, and certification for students enrolled in the Primary School Certificate (PSC), Junior School Certificate (JSC), and Secondary School Certificate (SSC) programs. Aside from conducting the PEC, JSC, and SSC examinations, the educational boards do not have a direct role in PVE. Still, they can collaborate with the Ministry of Education, Ministry of Home Affairs, police, and prison authorities to conduct and certify special education programs for VEO prison inmates of suspected VEOs who have dropped out of educational institutions.

(c) Bangladesh Open University

Bangladesh Open University (BOU) can help stop violent extremism (PVE) by giving radicalized groups a chance to get an alternative education and acquire new skills. BOU is the only university in the country that offers distance learning programs, providing students with flexible learning opportunities.

(d) Other Colleges and Universities

Intermediate and degree colleges and public and private universities should have provisions for their students to continue and finish their studies in prison. In Singapore, university faculty members can visit prisons to offer educational access to inmates willing to pursue their studies. Such in-person education and a mix of virtual classes can be organized for the prison-based VEOs in Bangladesh. Education through in-person classes should be fined for the remaining VEOs who are not in prison.

(e) Teachers and Trainers

Teachers and trainers can effectively prevent violent extremism by teaching students to think critically, be tolerant, and support their communities. They can also help people who have already become radicalized to recover and get back into society by making learning environments that are welcoming and supportive. Teachers and trainers can help build more inclusive and robust communities by giving good education and skills training (USIP 2017).

(f) Ministry of Home Affairs

Bangladesh's Ministry of Home Affairs can facilitate coordination between law enforcement and educational institutions. These programs may include counseling, educational opportunities, skill development, and other types of assistance. The ministry can also collaborate with other governmental agencies, civil society organizations, and communities to develop and implement these programs.

(g) CT Agencies

Among the CT agencies, the ATU, CTTC, and RAB may help VEOs by giving them access to education and skills training. They can hand over books, newspapers, guides, and other materials. They can also support their entrepreneurship aspirations and occasionally meet or follow up with them. They can also help other stakeholders with the reintegration policies, help them find jobs, and coordinate the counseling system.

(h) NGOs and CSOs

Various Bangladeshi NGOs and social organizations work on the policymaking and advising level; some help educate and rehabilitate VEOs. Some organizations can be brought under the collaborative platform. The foremost among them are BRAC and CAMPE, both of which have educational programs. Others, including the Manusher Jonno Foundation (MJF), Rupantor, and Institute for Informatics and Development (IID), can play a role. The field-level networks of MJF and Rupantor and the digital literacy capacity of IID can make a difference by introducing educational programs for the VEOs.

12.4 Key Activities

The following activities can be done to manage VEO rehabilitation through education.

(a) Access to education in the prisons

The prison authorities will arrange sessions on general education for convicted and under-trial detainees. The primary and secondary education boards will have policies and programs to recognize such learning opportunities. Those derailed from studies should be exposed to basic teachings of culture, ethics, mathematics, and language studies. The VEOs should be allowed to complete their PSC/JSC/SSC/HSC examinations. For religious education, the Madrasah Board will be part of the arrangements. A competent education board or the Bangladesh Open University shall conduct all certificate examinations (PSC/JSC/SSC/HSC or equivalent examinations for Madrasah). Similarly, undergraduate or graduate study opportunities can be made accessible to those willing to pursue their education in prisons.

(b) Develop institutional arrangements for ensuring access to education in the prisons

The MoHA (represented by ATU or CTTC) may sign an agreement/MoU with the Ministry of Education and the University Grants Commission to allow a select group of educational institutions to offer prison-based learning opportunities.

(c) Introduce life skills training

Skill training is also vital in this regard. The Police authorities can introduce professional trainers to VEOs who can offer training on various subjects. These include peace and social cohesion, non-violent communication, ethics, culture, etiquette, and soft skills. As for hard skills, they can be trained in information communication technology, public speaking, graphic designing, and computer coding, which will help them successfully re-integrate into society.

Authorities can encourage VEOs to read various Literature, Languages, and other similar subjects to broaden their horizons. They also need access to the library, newspaper, and computer. Internet courses provided by platforms such as EdX and Coursera can ensure good education and skills accreditation. The curriculum may introduce the topics of Physical Education and arts and crafts to facilitate creativity.

12.5 Methods of Operation

(a) For prison-based under-trial and convicted VEOs

Under-trial detainees may want to continue their incomplete studies while in prison. In such cases, detainees can enroll in specific educational programs that match their needs. They will also need books, tutors, and other support to pursue their studies. After finishing the courses, they will have opportunities to appear at assessment tests, including mid-term and final examinations. There may be unique and short courses on religion, ethics, and morality for the VEOs. Tutors can come to the prison under special arrangements with the prison authority and teach the detainees based on their status and needs.

(b) For under-trial detainees on bail

Under-trial detainees on bail can be enrolled in regular academic programs and continue their studies. They must regularly contact the CT agencies and report on the progress of their studies.

(c) For post-release VEOs

For school, college, madrasah, or university students convicted in a case and have finished their prison terms, CT agencies will encourage them to continue their studies. Financial support can cover their educational expenses if they have economic hardships. In such cases, tuition fees will be transferred to academic institutions, and students can receive some monthly stipends. The CT and intelligence agencies will periodically monitor released VEOs.

(d) For other beneficiaries

Educational opportunities shall be made available for other beneficiaries of deradicalization and rehabilitation, including the at-risk communities and those who have surrendered to the security forces but have not been imprisoned due to lack of substantive evidence or involvement in a significant offense.

12.6 Risks and Opportunities

Risks

- Assessing the educational needs and offering multiple streams of education for prison-based VEOs may be challenging due to a lack of resources.
- Some academic institutions or educators may be unwilling to interact with the VEO population, denying them a learning opportunity.
- Some VEOs may be unwilling to pursue mainstream education as they consider it not aligned with their religious dogma.

Opportunities

- CT agencies and the prison authorities in Bangladesh are well aware of the challenges of assessing the educational needs of imprisoned VEOs. Since the size of the VEO prison population is manageable, they can be brought under various academic and skills training programs.
- CT agencies will coordinate with educational institutions and educators to mitigate their concerns and encourage their active role in extending educational opportunities.
- The value of academic training as a path toward enlightenment will be projected. In addition, through family visits and religious and psychological counseling, VEOs will be encouraged to appreciate the value of formal education and training in enjoying a fulfilling life.

12.7 Monitoring and Evaluation Framework

(a) Lead Ministry

The Ministry of Education is the lead ministry. The Ministry of Education has two divisions: The Secondary and Higher Education Division (SHED) and the Technical and Madrasah Education Division (TMED). SHED and TMED, in consultation with the Public Security Division and the Security Services Division of the Ministry of Home Affairs, will develop, implement, and monitor policies relevant to ensuring educational opportunities for deradicalization and rehabilitation beneficiaries. Other concerned ministries, such as the Ministry of Women and Children Affairs, the Ministry of Youth and Sports, and the Ministry of Religious Affairs, can be brought on board due to cross-cutting issues of gender, youth, and religious studies.

(b) Lead Agency

Various CT agencies (ATU, CTTC, and RAB) will be responsible for monitoring the extent to which deradicalization beneficiaries attend schools and what challenges they confront. They will keep in contact with the families for monitoring purposes. Case officers from the Department of Social Services can also be appointed to maintain liaison between VEOs and CT agencies.

(c) Indicators

- Indicator 2: Numbers of VEOs enrolled in education and skills programs (with disaggregated data for various types of VEOs)
- Indicator 3: Number of VEOs who continued or finished their education and skills programs (with disaggregated data for multiple kinds of VEOs).

(d) Impact Assessment

Independent evaluators will conduct mid-term impact assessments regularly.

12.8 Conclusions

In conclusion, this chapter has emphasized the need for extending academic training for VEOs to help them reduce their vulnerability to extremist ideas and reintegrate into society. Resource shortages, educators' unwillingness, and VEOs' reluctance may appear to be some of the challenges. Opportunities exist to mitigate such challenges through concerted efforts and periodic monitoring by various stakeholders representing the education sector and CT agencies.

References

Khalil, J., Zeuthen, M., and Marsden, S. 2023. *A guide to deradicalisation and disengagement programming*. Centre for Research and Evidence on Security Threats.

Koehler, D., and Fiebig, V. 2019. *Knowing what to do: Academic and practitioner understanding of how to counter violent radicalization*. International Centre for Counter-Terrorism.

United States Institute of Peace. 2017. *Deradicalizing, rehabilitating, and reintegrating violent extremists: Lessons from the global community*. United States Institute of Peace.

Chapter 13
Vocational Skills Training

13.1 Introduction

This chapter analyses how technical and vocational training (TVET) can contribute to the deradicalization and rehabilitation of VEOs. Vocational training prepares VEOs to reintegrate into society by developing skills in income-generating activities. Such skills training would build self-confidence and self-esteem and complement other rehabilitative interventions by preparing individuals to walk away from the path of extremism (Marsden 2015).

13.2 Desired Outcomes

Various types of VEOs will receive vocational training free of charge, and after successful completion of a vocational skills training program, they will pursue gainful employment opportunities.

13.3 Key Actors

The government of Bangladesh has two types of vocational skills training providers who will be vital in offering vocational skills training to the VEOs. The list includes:

- Technical Schools and Colleges and the Polytechnic Institutes under the Department of Technical Education managed by the Ministry of Education
- Technical Training Centers (TTCs) under the Ministry of Expatriates' Welfare and Overseas Employment.

I. Ahmed et al., *Handbook on Deradicalization and Rehabilitation of Violent Extremist Offenders in Bangladesh*, SpringerBriefs in Environment, Security, Development and Peace 41, https://doi.org/10.1007/978-3-031-85807-9_13

In addition, various for-profit and non-profit skills training providers can help VEOs and their families become more skilled.

The CT agencies of Bangladesh Police (ATU, CTTC, and RAB) will partner with a select group of public, private, and non-profit TVET providers as part of a larger C/PVE strategy.

13.4 Key Activities

(a) Provide free TVET opportunities

The TVET providers, with financial support from the Government of Bangladesh, will offer free skills training programs in areas such as electrical and wiring, tailoring and dressmaking, masonry, carpentry, poultry, bakery and confectionery, and automotive. While many such skills training programs are currently in place for the general prison population, the under-trial or convicted VEOs in prisons need access to such programs (Silke 2011). As part of the VEO rehabilitation program, the prison authorities in Bangladesh (e.g., in high-security prisons, district jails, and central jails) will extend TVET opportunities to VEOs.

For the post-release VEOs, at-risk populations, and surrendered VEOs, the CT agencies will sign a memorandum of understanding with reputed TVET institutions to offer free skills training programs that match the student needs and the institutions' expertise. Family members of VEOs may also be considered eligible to participate in free TVET programs (Horgan and Braddock 2010).

(b) Provide skills certificates to successful participants

The TVET institutions conducting the training sessions shall assess trainees' performance and provide certificates of completion to successful trainees.

(c) Evaluate the long-term effect of skills training

A system will be in place to evaluate whether the skills training programs have any measurable effect on the course participants' ability to secure jobs and develop a respectful attitude toward society.

13.5 Methods of Operations

(a) Form a curriculum committee

CT agencies will collaborate with concerned stakeholders in the Ministry of Education and the Prisons Directorate to form a curriculum committee to determine a set of TVET programs for VEOs and at-risk populations.

(b) Create working groups for implementing TVET

Create two working groups: one for implementing TVET programs in prisons and the other for running such programs outside of prisons.

(c) Collaborate with TVET providers

CT agencies will collaborate with TVET institutions to assess the trainee's needs and to provide teaching-learning tools and other logistics. Prison authorities will create a referral system to ensure that all under-trial and convicted VEOs can enroll in the TVET programs on a rolling basis.

(d) Establish industry-linkages

The trainees will have opportunities for hands-on training in a select group of industries, allowing them to apply their theoretical knowledge to practice. Special arrangements will be made for trainees' short-term internship opportunities.

13.6 Risks and opportunities/Mitigation strategies

Risks

- o Some TVET institutions may be unwilling to enroll would-be or current VEOs, and a restrictive prison environment may create logistical challenges for some TVET programs to work in prison settings (El-Said 2015).
- o Trainers may have feelings of insecurity while interacting with the under-trial or convicted VEOs
- o Failure of monitoring would risk recidivism (Cherney 2018).

Opportunities

- o The CT agencies are willing to address the concerns of TVET institutions and work closely with them and the prison authorities to ensure that skills training opportunities run smoothly with the active participation of the VEOs and their families
- o Trainers with insecure feelings will have access to plain-clothes police protection. In prison facilities, correctional officers will take adequate measures to ensure trainers' and trainees' safety and security.
- o Security and intelligence agencies will closely monitor the VEOs' post-TVET training movement to reduce the risks of recidivism.

13.6.1 Monitoring and Evaluation Framework

(a) Lead Ministry

The Ministry of Home Affairs will lead in working closely with the Ministry of Education in developing TVET programs for the VEOs and at-risk populations. Due to the cross-cutting nature of gender and youth, the Ministry of Women and Children Affairs and the Ministry of Youth and Sports will also be included in inter-ministry coordination.

(b) Lead Agency

The CT agencies of Bangladesh Police, in collaboration with various security and intelligence agencies and the Prisons Authority, will manage the TVET programs for the VEOs.

(c) Indicators
- o Indicator 1: Numbers of participants enrolled in TVET programs
- o Indicator 3: Number of participants who finished the TVET programs

(d) Impact Assessment

Independent evaluators will assess periodic impact to determine whether TVET programs meet the desired outcomes.

13.7 Conclusion

A multi-stakeholder approach is needed to implement TVET programs for would-be or current VEOs. Some of the TVET programs may be on demand. In such a case, CT agencies and prison authorities must ensure a match between the demand and supply sides of skills training.

References

Horgan, J., and Braddock, K. 2010. Rehabilitating the terrorists?: Challenges in assessing the effectiveness of de-radicalization programs. *Terrorism and Political Violence* 22 (2): 267–291.

Marsden, S. V. 2015. *Reintegrating extremists: Deradicalisation and desistance.* Palgrave Macmillan.

Silke, A. 2011. Disengagement or deradicalization: A look at prison programs for jihadist terrorists. *CTC Sentinel* 4 (1): 18–21.

El-Said, H. 2015. *New approaches to countering terrorism: Designing and evaluating counter-radicalization and de-radicalization programs.* Palgrave Macmillan.

Cherney, A. 2018. Evaluating interventions to disengage extremist offenders: A study of the proactive integrated support model (PRISM). *Behavioral Sciences of Terrorism and Political Aggression* 10 (2): 1–20.

Chapter 14
Employment and Entrepreneurial Support

14.1 Introduction

Ensuring a productive livelihood opportunity is vital in any VEO rehabilitation and reintegration strategy. VEOs whose career path has been disrupted due to prison terms may find it hard to return to the job market and find employment. For VEOs who have not been imprisoned but lost their jobs due to allegations of involvement in VE activities or those who are unemployed will need to stop worrying about financial security for themselves and their families. Lack of livelihood opportunities may push them away from everyday life and allow violent extremist recruiters to exploit their situations. While concerned VEOs from various ideological bents and legal statuses may search for their livelihood opportunities, CT agencies must play an essentially facilitating role in ensuring that VEOs have access to meaningful income-generating activities and social stigma or past criminal records do not create stumbling blocks in their career paths.

14.2 Desired Outcome

Employment opportunities will be created, and entrepreneurial support will be given to VEOs. Imprisoned VEOs will receive these supports after they are released. Those not in prison and eligible to enter the job market should receive the support.

I. Ahmed et al., *Handbook on Deradicalization and Rehabilitation of Violent Extremist Offenders in Bangladesh*, SpringerBriefs in Environment, Security, Development and Peace 41, https://doi.org/10.1007/978-3-031-85807-9_14

14.3 Key Actors

Business chambers, prison authorities, and Bangladesh Police are critical actors in implementing this economic component of the VEO rehabilitation and reintegration strategy. There is a precise distribution of responsibilities among the key actors. Among the business chambers, the Bangladesh Garment Manufacturers and Exporters Association (BGMEA), the Bangladesh Knitwear Manufacturers Association (BKMEA), and the Federation of Bangladesh Chambers of Commerce and Industries (FBCCI) are expected to play a critical role in developing a system for job placement of eligible VEOs. Bangladesh Academy for Rural Development (BARD) can be brought on board to design career opportunities for VEOs with a farming background who wish to engage in agricultural activities. Bangladesh Association for Software and Information Services (BASIS) can join the initiative to extend employment and entrepreneurial opportunities for those requisite academic backgrounds, professional skills, and career interests in the information technology sector.

Among various units of Bangladesh Police, the ATU and the CTTC will have dedicated focal persons to maintain liaison with the business chambers to manage the economic component of VEO rehabilitation.

14.4 Key Activities

(a) Establish a VEO Job Center under the guidance of CT Agencies (ATU, CTTC, and RAB) to offer professional counseling

Concerned CT agencies in Bangladesh (e.g., ATU and CTTC) implementing the VEO deradicalization and rehabilitation program will establish a VEO Job Center to offer professional career counseling and job placement services to prospective VEOs seeking employment and entrepreneurial support. The Job Center will be resourced by full-time personnel with a background in human resource management, enterprise development, and business administration. The VEO Job Center will maintain a database of VEOs willing to receive skills training and employment/entrepreneurial support. The database will compile information about the VEO's academic and professional background, skills acquired, financial status, and preferred livelihood opportunity plans. The Job Center staff will conduct a Needs Assessment for Economic Rehabilitation to match the demand and supply sides (Appendix 2).

(b) Connect with the industries and financial institutions to facilitate VEO's income-generating activities

VEOs must connect with industries and financial institutions to find jobs and secure seed money for enterprise development. CT agencies will partner with various companies' human resources (HR) sections to arrange job placement by matching the demand and supply sides. VEOs wishing to engage in farming activities will be connected to agricultural extension officers at the field levels to do a needs assessment and provide the requisite support.

(c) Create a system for employers to communicate with the CT agencies (ATU, CTTC) to share concerns, report positive or negative behavioral changes, and assess security risks

Private firms hiring VEOs shall communicate with CT agencies to share their concerns, report positive or negative behavioral changes, and assess security risks. The outputs of such communication will be used in the Risks and Need Assessment for each VEO rehabilitation service recipient.

(d) Take stock of prior economic rehabilitation programs and compare the results of past and present programs

There is a need for taking stock of past economic rehabilitation programs, including those for the ethno-nationalist rebels in the Chattogram Hill Tracts (CHT), Ultra left militants in the north-western and south-western districts, and faith-based militants around the country (Ahmmed et al. 2013; Bashar 2011; Chakma 2014, 2017; Islam and Chakma 2013; Salam and Aktar 2014). In most cases, the VEOs received either one-time cash support or food stamps, community farming, or job Placement in the lower ranks of civilian police and auxiliary force Ansar and Village Development Party. No systematic impact assessment has been done to review the results of such economic rehabilitation initiatives. CT agencies overseeing the current VEO rehabilitation and reintegration program should take stock of past efforts and compare their impacts with the outcomes of recent initiatives.

14.5 Methods of Operation

(a) Organize a job fair to offer job and entrepreneurial counseling

The VEO Job Center will organize a job fair to offer job and placement and entrepreneurial counseling. The job fair can be arranged at a place mutually agreed upon by the CT agencies and the business chambers. Business chambers will be encouraged to sponsor such events as part of their corporate social responsibility.

(b) VEO Job Center will connect representatives from various professional sectors, such as BGMEA, BKMEA, FBCCI, and other professional bodies

The RMG industry is Bangladesh's most significant foreign currency source, with a massive demand for skilled human resources. The Job Center can connect VEO rehabilitation program participants interested in pursuing a career in the RMG industry with BGMEA and BKMEA to find a job. As stated, the Job Center can join the FBCCI, BASIS, and BARD as needed. The Job Center will share the biodata of VEO job seekers with prospective employers and their associations, arrange interviews, and keep job placement records.

(c) Financial institutions/Banks can offer accessible loan facilities to encourage them to do business

The VEO Job Center will collaborate with the Bangladesh Association of Bankers to develop loan and grant products for VEOs interested in enterprise development and needing seed money. The Bangladesh Bank can request commercial banks to arrange small and medium enterprise (SME) loans to facilitate businesses owned by rehabilitated VEOs.

(d) The Job Center can also facilitate trade licensing and other regulatory documents

The VEO Job Center will facilitate the issuing of trade licenses for VEOs interested in self-employment or SME businesses. It will collaborate with city corporations, municipalities, and other local government bodies that have the mandate to issue the licenses.

14.6 Risks and Opportunities/Mitigation Strategies

Risks

- o Some employers may be unwilling or unable to find a job for a VEO.
- o Some financial institutions may be reluctant to offer loan packages to VEOS.
- o Some VEOs may be unwilling to join any jobs arranged by the VEO JOB Center, fearing backlash and constant monitoring.
- o Some VEOs may re-engage in VE activities even after a job.

Opportunities

Various business chambers and employers' associations (e.g., BGMEA, BKMEA, and FBCCI) are interested in partnering with CT agencies to counter and prevent violent extremism in various capacities. These include creating skills training and livelihood opportunities for VEOs. The Bankers' Association BAB has also shown a positive interest in arranging SME loans for VEO rehabilitation. CT agencies know VEOs' concerns about extensive monitoring and potential harassment. Following the Indonesian model, CT agencies must engage rehabilitated former militants to create trust and confidence in the rehabilitation program. Local NGOs with extensive field-level operations will also be invited to engage the VEOs and reduce their chances of re-engagement in VE activities. Finally, CT agencies have a consensus on employment support for VEOs and mitigating any risks that may arise in implementing economic rehabilitation initiatives.

14.7 Monitoring and Evaluation Framework

(a) Lead Ministry

The Ministry of Home Affairs (MOHA) will take the lead. Other concerned ministries include the Ministry of Agriculture, the Ministry of Commerce (MOC), the Ministry of Industries (MOI), the Ministry of Labor and Employment (MOLE), the Ministry of Youth & Sports (MOYS); and the Ministry of Women and Children Affairs (MOWCA) will provide necessary supports. The following is the planned distribution of responsibilities among the ministries:

- MOHA: Overall supervision
- MOA, MOC, and MOI: Job creation
- MOLE & MOYS: Decent work conditions and skill training
- MOWCA: Gender sensitivity and women's rights

(b) Lead Agency

Bangladesh Police (ATU, CTTC, and RAB) will manage the VEO rehabilitation and reintegration programs in collaboration with various security and intelligence agencies and the Prisons Authority.

(c) Indicator

Two indicators will be used to monitor and evaluate the Employment and Entrepreneurial Support:

- Indicator 1: Yearly number of VEOs applying for employment and entrepreneurial support from the Job Center
- Indicator 2: Yearly Number of VEOs receiving employment and entrepreneurial support from the Job Center

(d) Impact Assessment

Independent evaluators will conduct a mid-term impact assessment in the 3rd year and an end-term impact assessment in the 4th year.

14.8 Conclusion

This chapter has stressed that a secure livelihood opportunity is imperative for successful VEO rehabilitation and reintegration. CT agencies must create a dedicated VEO Job Center and partner with various employers' associations and agencies to provide employment and entrepreneurial support to VEOs who cannot find a job themselves. Skills training and funding are both critical. Risks may arise in achieving the desired goal of ensuring economic security for the VEOs. Scopes for mitigating the risks exist. Inter-ministerial coordination is essential, but the CT agencies will take the lead in implementing the activities related to the economic pathways to VEO rehabilitation and reintegration.

Appendix 2: Needs Assessment for Economic Rehabilitation

<table>
<tr><td colspan="4">Name of Beneficiary</td></tr>
<tr><td>Gender</td><td>Male</td><td>Female</td><td>Trans-gendered</td></tr>
<tr><td>Academic Background</td><td colspan="3">(a) No formal education
(b) Completed 5th grade
(c) Completed 8th grade
(d)Completed 10th grade
(e) Completed 12th grade
(f) Completed undergraduate degree
(g) Completed postgraduate degree</td></tr>
<tr><td>Professional Background</td><td colspan="3">(a) Was previously employed
(b) Was never employed</td></tr>
<tr><td>Skills Training Certificate</td><td colspan="3">(a) Completed a Skills Training Course
(b) Did not complete any Skills Training Course
(c) Acquired practical work experiences and need Recognition of Prior Skills (RPL)</td></tr>
<tr><td>Preferred livelihood option</td><td colspan="3">(a) Agriculture
(b) Business
(c) Service Sector
(d) Others</td></tr>
<tr><td>What kind of jobs did you have before?</td><td colspan="3">(a) Private Service
(b) Public Service
(c) Business
(d) Farming
(e) Self-employed
(f) Others</td></tr>
<tr><td>What kind of jobs have you tried recently?</td><td colspan="3">Mention any three:</td></tr>
<tr><td>What do you think are the key challenges to getting a job?</td><td colspan="3">Mention any three:</td></tr>
<tr><td>Do you need skills training support?</td><td colspan="3">(a) Yes
(b) No
If yes, please specify</td></tr>
<tr><td>Do you need any job placement support?</td><td colspan="3">(a) Yes
(b) No
If yes, please specify what kind of job</td></tr>
<tr><td>Do you need any seed money for stating a small and medium enterprise?</td><td colspan="3">(a) Yes
(b) No</td></tr>
<tr><td>Overall Assessment</td><td colspan="3">The candidate can be given:
(a) Employment support
(b) Entrepreneurial support
(c) No support</td></tr>
</table>

References

Ahmmed, Helal Uddin, Md Matiul Hoque Masud, Md Faisal, and Md Niaz Morshed. 2013. "The Chittagong Hill Tracts Peace Accord in Bangladesh: An Overview." *Mediterranean Journal of Social Sciences* 4 (4): 123-130.

Bashar, Iftekharul. 2011. "Bangladesh's Forgotten Crisis: land, ethnicity, and violence in the Chittagong Hill Tracts." *Counter Terrorist Trends and Analyses* 3 (4): 1-5.

Chakma, Ananda Bikash. 2014. "Peacebuilding in the Chittagong Hill Tracts (CHT): An institutionalist approach." *Journal of the Asiatic Society of Bangladesh* 59 (1): 111-138.

Chakma, Anurug. 2017. "The Peacebuilding of the Chittagong Hill Tracts (CHT), Bangladesh: Donor-Driven or Demand-Driven?" *Asian Journal of Peacebuilding* 5 (2): 223-242.

Islam, R., and Anurug Chakma. 2013. "Major Obstacles to the Process of Implementing Peace: Experience from Chittagong Hill Tracts (CHT) in Bangladesh." *Peace and Conflict Review* 7 (2): 29-46.

Salam, Mohammad Fakhrus, and Hajera Aktar. 2014. "Ethnic problems in Bangladesh: a study of Chittagong Hill tracts." *SUST Journal of Social Sciences* 22 (2): 53-63.

Chapter 15
Support for the Family and Community Members

15.1 Introduction

Family members of the violent extremist offenders (VEOs) and the community gatekeepers from the neighborhood play crucial roles in the deradicalization and rehabilitation programs of the VEOs. This chapter demonstrates how government and non-government agencies consider several interventions to make the family members and community gatekeepers aware of the activities of the convicted and post-release VEOs. Family and community members can also play proactive roles in counter-radicalization by addressing issues regarding at-risk communities. Their collaboration can also support the prevention activities of CTTC and other counter-terrorism forces.

15.2 Desired Outcome

VEOs' families and communities will receive various support to collaborate with the government, private sector, and civil society to make their social reintegration successful.

15.3 Key Actors

(a) CT agencies of Bangladesh Police

As part of their regular C/PVE programs, the CT agencies of Bangladesh Police can provide support to the families and communities affected by violent extremism. The ultimate goal is to promote peace, stability, and reintegration into society.

I. Ahmed et al., *Handbook on Deradicalization and Rehabilitation of Violent Extremist Offenders in Bangladesh*, SpringerBriefs in Environment, Security, Development and Peace 41, https://doi.org/10.1007/978-3-031-85807-9_15

(b) Civil society organizations (CSOs)

CSOs will provide counseling and mental health services to boost emotional and psychological well-being. They can provide community education and outreach programs for at-risk communities and family members. They facilitate education and job training programs to help family and community members acquire skills and knowledge. CSOs can also provide financial assistance and build social connections between people committed to peace, non-violence, and community development.

(c) Religious clerics and scholars

Religious clerics and scholars will provide spiritual and moral guidance to families and communities impacted by violent extremism, helping promote values of peace, compassion, and understanding. They can also promote peace and non-violence by using their influence. By working with families, communities, civil society organizations, and government agencies, religious clerics can help create a supportive and inclusive environment that promotes peace, non-violence, and the successful rehabilitation of violent extremists.

(d) Psychological Counsellors

Psychological counsellors will be essential in supporting the family and community members of violent extremists. They will provide emotional support and coping strategies to help them process their experiences and feelings related to extremist behavior. They will also work with families and communities to address any stigmatization and discrimination they may face and support their reintegration into society.

(e) Educational Institutions

Educational institutions will provide free and formal education to the immediate family members (children) of the VEOs who come from low-income families and cannot afford the cost of education. Schools and madrasahs will be encouraged to offer lessons on tolerance, diversity, and critical thinking in children's minds. Teachers can encourage students to talk about sensitive topics openly and respectfully, giving them opportunities to do community service and other activities that unite people.

Colleges and universities can offer research and training programs to help people learn more about the causes and effects of violent extremism, find ways to stop it and help people already involved. As part of the community, the universities can also help students, staff, and faculty who have been hurt by extremism by providing support services.

15.4 Key Activities

(a) Build trust among various stakeholders

Building trust is critical in family and community reintegration, and trust-building may take time. So, the plans should be long-term and in conjunction with other support activities for the former convicted VEOs. A VEO can come from a family with complex problems that may need various support modes. Intelligence services, police, child welfare and social welfare agencies, employment agencies, local authorities, community organizations, judicial support, and prison authorities will all be involved. Sometimes, the offender may find out their family has helped law enforcement apprehend them. This can cause relationship tensions within the family. Cooperation between the prison authorities and other actors is necessary for family and community reintegration. The media may approach family members to publish stories or study cases. If the family members of a VEO share similar extremist ideology, they must require deradicalization support.

(b) Assess the motives of families and communities

CT agencies will assess the motives of families and communities of VEOs. Some families may show positive attitudes by welcoming the offer of support, visiting the VEOs in prisons, and understanding that they can be part of the solution. Others may show negative attitudes and be skeptical of deradicalization and rehabilitation.

(c) Build new social networks for VEOs

The 'terrorist' label may make it difficult for VEOs to socialize with other people. For them, mentors and support professionals may be the only social connections. In such a context, going to new places, participating in leisurely group activities, and pursuing educational/vocational training can help an individual meet new people and build new connections. While forming new relationships, the VEO should not be pressured to talk about their past, even though the support partners would know from the program officials.

(d) Restore healthy family dynamics

The families of VEOs may come from diverse social, political, and geographical backgrounds. A family support provider (local CSO member trained on the matter) should recognize that family members have different priorities, dreams, and goals that should be respected and balanced for a healthy family system. Parents need mental support to play a vital role in rehabilitating the VEO and restoring the family bondage. Helping the family with issues, psychological challenges, and mental illnesses is also necessary. Families of under-trial and convicted detainees will need information about the legal proceedings and prison situation so that everyone can get a sense of hope and connection.

(e) Establishing information-sharing protocols

All the stakeholders—support providers and the beneficiary families and community members—need to be able to share information. The family should be able to contact the police in case of security risk. Support workers should have colleagues with whom they can confidentially discuss issues, including their security risks, and receive help from security services if needed to ensure the health and safety of professionals. A safe space to discuss complex cases and a safety protocol to protect their needs need to be established for the optimum performance of family support professionals. Support professionals should not be from the same community, as the family members may feel intimidated.

(f) Community engagement

The local government, like the Union Council and Ward Council, local elders, religious leaders like Imams, Muazzins, and members of mosque management committees, and public service providers such as teachers and healthcare providers are essential leaders and gatekeepers in the broader community outside the family. Engaging with them through discussions and awareness programs about VEO rehabilitation can make them more accepting of the individual. At-risk members of the community can be identified and engaged in the deradicalization process. Awareness and acceptance are critical interventions for community support. Friends and neighbors of the VEO may be important sources of information and support in community rehabilitation (Hussin 2018; Gunaratna 2017).

15.5 Methods of Operation

(a) For Under-trial detainees (on bail and in prison)

Families of prisoners awaiting trial can play an essential role in their rehabilitation and reintegration into society. They help provide emotional and psychological support by ensuring a caring and nurturing atmosphere that allows the VEOs to cope with the judicial process and detention stress. They can support VEOs' access to education and training programs that will assist them in acquiring the skills and knowledge required for reintegration into society. Moreover, the family can encourage the detainee to connect positively with those committed to peace, nonviolence, and community development. The family can argue for the under-trial detainees' fair treatment and support their legal rights.

(b) For convicted detainees (in prison)

First, psychological support is essential for the families and community members of convicted VEOs. This can involve counseling, guidance, and support to help them process their emotions, understand the offender's behavior, and cope with the consequences of the offender's actions. Then, it is essential to foster an open dialogue.

Second, it is crucial to foster an open dialogue between the family, the offender, and the community. This can help create an environment of understanding and support and build trust between all parties.

Third, one may consider educating the community about violent extremism and the rehabilitation of VEOs. This can help create a broader understanding and acceptance of the offender and their rehabilitation process. Developing programs that facilitate the reintegration of VEOs into their communities is a must. These programs should provide education, job training, and other resources to help offenders reintegrate into society.

Last but not least, it is vital to support victims of violent extremism. This can involve counseling, financial assistance, and other services to help them cope with their experiences and move forward.

(c) For post-release VEOs

Acceptance from the broader community may challenge the VEO and the VEO's family in the post-release scenario. Discussing and raising awareness about the changed behavior of a rehabilitee can help them reintegrate into the social network. Family counseling can be one of the ways to provide such support. Both psychological and religious counseling may be needed for the families. Family members should be able to contact rehabilitation agencies for help in emergencies. Spouses and children of the VEOs may require special attention as they may face ostracization, alienation, and subsequent risk of radicalization.

Community leaders such as teachers, religious clerics (imams, madrassah scholars), and local politicians (ward counselors, union chairpersons, and village elders play crucial roles in the rehabilitation process. Community gatekeepers are the most important among the leaders as they control others' access to VEO rehabilitation support. Family elders, heads of families, local imams, and political leaders are essential gatekeepers who can either facilitate or hamper reintegration. Schools where the children of VEOs attend may also need to be informed.

Thus, the main activities to provide support for the families of post-release VEOs are:

(a) Organize meetings with the family members and extended family of the VEO to inform them,
(b) Organize family counseling (psychological and religious) sessions to assess needs and provide support based on the assessment,
(c) Organize *Uthan Boithok* (Yard Meeting) once a month with the community leaders and gatekeepers (Family elders, heads of families, local imams, local political leaders, and schoolteachers) to create support networks. The local police station, in collaboration with CTTC, will monitor the tasks as necessary.

15.6 Risks and Opportunities

Risks

- o Family and community members of VEOs may face stigma and discrimination, making them unwilling to cooperate with the rehabilitation programs.
- o VEOs may radicalize their family and community members by exposing them to their extremist ideology and behavior.
- o Family and community members may be reluctant to report suspicious activity or behavior of VEOs, fearing legal implications for them.
- o Family and community members may be vulnerable to retaliatory violence and intimidation from VEOs.

Opportunities

- o CT agencies and CSOs will support family and community members of VEOs to create a buffer to prevent radicalization and recruitment into violent extremist groups.
- o CT agencies and CSOs will work with families and communities to disrupt the cycle of radicalization and violence by providing alternative means of support and counseling.
- o CT agencies will create a safe and supportive environment for family and community members so that they can report suspicious activity or behavior of VEOs.
- o CT agencies will help to strengthen the resilience of family and community members to resist the influence of violent extremist ideologies and behaviors.

15.6.1 Monitoring and Evaluation Framework

(a) Lead Ministry

The Ministry of Home Affairs will take the lead. Other concerned ministries, including the Ministry of Social Welfare, the Ministry of Youth & Sports (MOYS), and the Ministry of Women and Children Affairs, will play a support role. The following is the planned distribution of responsibilities among the ministries:

- o MOHA: Overall coordination
- o MOSW: Coordination with NGOs and CSO
- o MOYs: Engagement of youth clubs
- o MOWCA: Gender sensitivity and women's rights

(b) Lead Agency

The CT agencies of Bangladesh Police (ATU, CTTC, and RAB), in collaboration with various security and intelligence agencies and the Prisons Authority, will manage the support services for the families and communities of VEOs.

(c) Indicators

- o Indicator 1: Number of family units enrolled in a support system
- o Indicator 2: Number of communities enrolled in a support system
- o Indicator 3: Number of family units cooperated with CT agencies implementing rehabilitation programs
- o Indicator 4: Number of communities cooperated with CT agencies implementing rehabilitation programs

(d) Impact Assessment

Independent evaluators will conduct a periodic impact assessment. Based on the impact assessment, the support will be adjusted to VEO families and communities based on the analysis's findings. Finally, CT agencies will implement corrective actions as necessary to ensure the support provided to VEO families and communities is effective and sustainable.

15.7 Conclusion

It is imperative to support family and community members of VEOs to help create a suitable environment for their deradicalization, facilitating their social reintegration process. It is crucial to recognize that rehabilitation is a challenging process and that not all violent extremists may be willing or able to participate in rehabilitation programs. By working together, families, communities, civil society organizations, and government agencies can provide the support and resources needed to help violent extremists successfully reintegrate into society and lead peaceful and productive lives.

References

Gunaratna, Rohan. 2017. "Global Terrorist Rehabilitation and Community Engagement Programmes: The State-of-the-art." Paper presented at the 167th United Nations Asia and Far East Institute for the Prevention of Crime and the Treatment of Offenders (UNAFEI) International Training Course.

Hussin, Sabariah M. 2018. *Strategic Counterterrorism, Terrorist Rehabilitation, and Community Engagement: The Singapore Experience.* 167th United Nations Asia and Far East Institute for the Prevention of Crime and the Treatment of Offenders (UNAFEI) International Training Course Visiting Experts' Papers. Resource Material Series No. 104. Tokyo: UNAFEI.

Chapter 16
Resettlement Support

16.1 Introduction

Resettlement support may often become necessary in rehabilitating VEOs. Resettlement primarily refers to the community placement of a VEO with their family members, most preferably in a new area. It may need to be supported by financial and other resources. This is a multi-stakeholder support scheme. This chapter elaborates on the resettlement support for post-released VEOs who volunteered and showed promising features for reintegration with society.

16.2 Desired Outcome

The VEOs, after completing their prison terms and being released from there, will be resettled in a new area and reintegrated into society in a way that allows them to participate in local societal and economic activities without a sense of deprivation or stigma (Horgan and Braddock 2010). If there is a need, physical resettlement is the primary objective of such interventions. Nonetheless, it is a part of the broader rehabilitation process, where physical resettlement is supported by psychological, religious counseling, and other socio-economic support services (Neumann 2010).

The resettlement process will help CT agencies monitor the progress of deradicalization and rehabilitation of VEOs. Furthermore, based on the success of the holistic approach to deradicalization, the former VEOs may become a voice against terrorism or violent extremism (in possible cases) and assist the police authority in pertinent situations (Marsden 2017).

I. Ahmed et al., *Handbook on Deradicalization and Rehabilitation of Violent Extremist Offenders in Bangladesh*, SpringerBriefs in Environment, Security, Development and Peace 41, https://doi.org/10.1007/978-3-031-85807-9_16

16.3 Key Actors

(a) CT Agencies

The CTTC is the focal point of resettlement activity. As the CTTC maintains a database of VEOs, their conviction status, background, and family history, they can design the physical resettlement plan.

(b) Ministry of Youth and Sports

The Ministry's Youth Directorate will coordinate and assist the CTTC in providing other skills-based support to the target group and resettlements.

(c) Ministry of Land

The Ministry of Land will prepare a list of unused lands in different communities, or it may ensure a living space for the family of the former convicted VEO if they have no other place to go.

(d) NGOs and CSOs

ATU and CTTC can collaborate with a national NGO with experience managing displacement-induced resettlement of families. The NGO/s can provide administrative assistance to the families and disburse financial resources where necessary.

16.4 Key Activities

(a) Conduct an assessment of resettlement needs

Prepare a list of VEOs who have declared the need for physical resettlement to a community different from their previous habitat.

(b) Provide resettlement support to families of VEOs

The former VEO may want to resettle alone or with the family. The CT agencies will encourage the family's resettlement. After a team assesses security and support services professionals, the resettlement may occur in a suitable place.

(c) Provide financial support

Livelihood opportunities must be given to the released VEOs. These include financial support, livestock, housing, and the like;

(d) Provide social reintegration support

The role of local communities is critical. With the help of psychologists and security professionals, a code of conduct will be developed to avoid social stigma for the VEOs and their families.

(e) Conduct monitoring and surveillance

CT Agencies & local LEAs will monitor the movement of released VEOs to prevent their re-engagement with extremist groups.

16.5 Methods of Operations

This section discusses the methods of operation for the resettlement of post-release VEOs.

(a) Physical resettlement

The CT agencies and the concerned NGOs will prepare a list of communities and make a list of compatibility for resettlement based on the list of the VEOs. In a society where the released VEO will be resettled, local police and civil administration may need to be sensitized for practical cooperation. The VEOs require some one-time seed cash to restart their new lives in an unknown area. An employment opportunity will indeed strengthen the success of resettlement.

(b) Social reintegration support

Besides other stakeholders, local police can also play a vital role in avoiding social stigma for the post-released VEOs and their family members. It is the local police who will certify that the person was related to VE (terrorism) activities, but they are now repented and required to be rehabilitated into society. Hiding information regarding the linkage to terrorism or violent extremism might backfire in the long run as there is the risk of re-radicalization of the post-released VEOs. Also, having the police on the side of the post-released VEOs will give them an excellent footing for social acceptance.

(c) Monitoring and Surveillance

The monitoring and surveillance need to be done in several layers, as described below:

First, ATU and CTTC will maintain a record of the post-released VEOs (who have finished prison tenure regarding terrorism cases). However, this record is kept only for Kerniganj and Kashimpur prisons. It is essential to extend the initiative to all the prisons of Bangladesh. CTTC and ATU can maintain this record, increasing its accuracy and facilitating verification.

Second, based on the gravity of the charges, ATU and CTTC or any competent law enforcement agency can monitor a single post-released VEO. Also, this will require greater cooperation between the two agencies. According to the existing law, CTTC is mandated to work within Dhaka city, and ATU has been empowered to work all over Bangladesh. Using this boundary of law, CTTC can monitor the activities of the post-released VEOs within the capital city. In contrast, ATU can cover the rest of Bangladesh and some important ones within Dhaka.

Third, ATU and CTTC will designate one police officer who will communicate with the VEO, their family, and the local police station in that particular case.

Fourth, CTTC and ATU will communicate regularly with local police to get updates on the VEOs. They will also need to arrange district- and division-wise seminars with police personnel to keep the higher authority updated on the monitoring and surveillance situation.

Fifth, the time demands a central digital database on the number of post-released VEOs, bailed and acquitted ones. This database will be accessible only by designated ATU or CTTC personnel. Creating such a central database is essential as the nature of the police job in Bangladesh requires an officer (ASP upwards) to shift their work every two to three years. However, there are some exceptions, and the new workstation might not be designated to deal with issues such as terrorism or violent extremism. As a result, when a new officer joins the ATU or CTTC, they can use the database to continue monitoring and surveillance.

Finally, Bangladesh Police is permitted to obtain information from village police (which is also termed as rural police or Gram Police) by the Police Regulation of Bengal (PRB) sections 32, 51, 60(c(i)), 362(c), 365, and 370. Villages are the smallest unit (most minor human settlements) of Bangladesh, and the rural police members are located in every village. The positioning of the village police or Gram Police is a huge opportunity to collect information from them, and according to section 370 of the PRB, the local police can demand information from the village police on specific issues, including the movement of particular persons (370 (X), (Xi)). The local police must utilize this authority to ensure proper surveillance of the post-released VEOs.

(d) Reporting procedure

The local police and the deradicalization centers will be under ATU and CTTC in case of monitoring and surveillance of the post-released VEOs. The local police will submit reports to ATU and CTTC every three months on the present whereabouts and livelihood of the post-released VEOs. The local police will also be bound to provide information on short notice in exceptional cases. The deradicalization center will report on the mental state of the VEOs annually directly to ATU and CTTC. The deradicalization center will continue this process for seven consecutive years, and if the report remains positive (that means the person remains deradicalized), the deradicalization center will discontinue the information.

The police station will prepare initial monitoring reports with help from local inhabitants, sources, and village police (Gram Police). After three months of compiling, these reports will be prepared monthly and sent to ATU and CTTC. Also, the village police (Gram Police) will inform the local police immediately if any suspicious activities regarding the VEOs are observed or if the village police suspect some omen.

16.6 Risks and Opportunities

Risks

- There is always the risk that a post-released VEO might be re-radicalized,
- A community may not accept a new person or a family who had a traumatized past,
- The scarcity of resources for proper resettlement,
- The CT police (including special units like ATU and CTTC) and other agencies may suffer from a deficiency of coordination.

Opportunities

The following opportunities exist to mitigate the risks:

- First, when the local authority resettles a post-released VEO, the local police will certify that the person was engaged in VE activities. Still, they have repented, and now, with proper assurance from the VEO, they must be allowed to be reintegrated into society as they have committed not to turn to VE and will help the police whenever required.
- Also, the police (with the help of ATU and CTTC) will inform the local inhabitants how the person has helped find the other accused of the case or cases and how this has made society more secure. This will have two effects. On the one hand, it will help the post-released VEOs to gain local trust. On the other hand, the members of the terrorist organizations will distrust them (post-released VEO) forever, which will curb the possibility of re-radicalization in the long run. Such controlling facts, along with surveillance from local and special police units (ATU and CTTC), will lower the possibility of re-radicalization of the post-released VEOs.

16.7 Monitoring and Evaluation Framework

(a) Lead Ministry

The Ministry of Home Affairs is the lead ministry managing the post-release resettlement of VEOs.

(b) Lead Agency

The monitoring authority must remain within the police to ensure that the post-released VEO is not re-radicalized or engaged in other violent activities. ATU and CTTC will be in the upper tier of the monitoring. The organization (ATU or CTTC) that monitors a particular VEO needs to prepare a sixth monthly report and send it to the police headquarters for observation and preservation. There needs to be a committee at the police headquarters that will oversee the whole process without interruption and work at the top of the monitoring layer.

Indicators:

- Indicator 1: Number of VEOs released after the prison term
- Indicator 2: Number of VEOs resettled
- Indicator 3: Patterns of other supports (finance) to facilitate resettlement,
- Indicator 4: Number of VEOs and others who left the program stayed permanently.

(d) Impact Assessment:

Independent evaluators will have access to data to assess the impact of the resettlement of released VEOs.

16.8 Conclusion

This chapter analyzed the process of resettlement support to be offered to VEOs who have finished their prison terms and have walked out of prison as free citizens. If social stigma and other challenges compel released VEOs to relocate and resettle in a community of their choice, CT agencies will provide such support. CT agencies will collaborate with local police to receive timely updates on the resettlement status of released VEOs.

References

Horgan, J., and Braddock, K. 2010. Rehabilitating the terrorists?: Challenges in assessing the effectiveness of de-radicalization programs. *Terrorism and Political Violence* 22 (2): 267–291.

Marsden, S. V. 2017. *Reintegrating extremists: Deradicalisation and desistance*. Palgrave Macmillan.

Neumann, P. R. 2010. *Prisons and terrorism: Radicalisation and de-radicalisation in 15 countries*. International Centre for the Study of Radicalisation and Political Violence.

Part IV
Policy Issues

Chapter 17
Policy Reforms

17.1 Introduction

This chapter analyzes the scope for legal and policy reforms in implementing VEO deradicalization and rehabilitation in Bangladesh. It argues that legal and policy reforms may take various routes. The Ministry of Home Affairs will lead the process of reforms, which involves multi-stakeholder consultation. It discusses the risks and opportunities and a monitoring and evaluation system for legal and policy reforms.

17.2 Desired Outcome

Bangladesh's VEO deradicalization and rehabilitation programs are implemented with a clear legal footing and necessary policy guidelines. The legal base and policy procedures may be in one of the following forms:

(a) Passing a new full-fledged law for VEO deradicalization and rehabilitation;
(b) Include VEO deradicalization and rehabilitation in a National C/PVE/CT Strategy and
(c) If the process for legal reform or passage of a new law is delayed, the Ministry of Home Affairs can issue a National Strategy to start the VEO deradicalization and rehabilitation (read some examples of national strategies, White House 2018; Zhou 2019).

I. Ahmed et al., *Handbook on Deradicalization and Rehabilitation of Violent Extremist Offenders in Bangladesh*, SpringerBriefs in Environment, Security, Development and Peace 41, https://doi.org/10.1007/978-3-031-85807-9_17

17.3 Key Actors

The Ministry of Home Affairs (MOHA) is the lead ministry of the government of Bangladesh in countering and preventing violent extremism (C/PVE). MOHA operates with two divisions: the Public Security Division (PSD) and the Security Services Division (SSD). Regarding the VEO deradicalization and rehabilitation, two key operational actors are the Bangladesh Police and the Prisons Directorate. As stated earlier in this Handbook, C/PVE responsibilities are distributed among various police entities, including the Anti Terrorism Unit (ATU) and the Counter Terrorism and Transnational Crime (CTTC) Unit of Dhaka Metropolitan Police. Under-trial and convicted VEOs are primarily concentrated in the Kashimpur High-Security Prison Unit, and a few are housed in various district and central jails. The law enforcement agencies report to the PSD, while the prison authorities report to the SSD of MOHA. This stakeholder mapping is crucial for understanding that substantive inputs from Bangladesh Police and Bangladesh Prisons Directorate should inform legal and policy reforms for VEO deradicalization and rehabilitation.

A multi-stakeholder drafting committee shall amend the Anti-Terrorism Act 2009 to include provisions relevant to VEO deradicalization and rehabilitation. The drafting committee will comprise MOHA delegates (PSD and SSD), Police HQ, ATU, CTTC, Rapid Action Battalion, Prisons Directorate, Kashimpur High-Security Prison Unit, legal and judicial experts, criminologists, security and counterterrorism analysts, gender and human rights experts. An inter-ministerial meeting will be needed to vet and fine-tune the draft. The draft shall be placed in the Cabinet Meeting for approval before it is placed in the *Jatiya Sangsad* (National Parliament of Bangladesh) for parliamentary approval.

17.4 Key Activities

(a) Draft a Policy Directive/Legal Amendment/National Strategy for VEO Deradicalization and Rehabilitation

Bangladesh lacks any written legal and policy instrument for VEO deradicalization and rehabilitation. Hence, drafting a legal and policy directive would be critical in addressing this lacuna. The draft should draw inspiration from a culture of inclusion and tolerance and comply with international standards and best practices.[1]

(b) Provide Capacity Building Training

Provide capacity-building training to various deradicalization and rehabilitation practitioners so that they can comply with legal and policy guidelines. The CT agencies

[1] These include the best practices developed by the Global Counter Terrorism Forum and the UNODC, amongst others.

(ATU and CTTC) will take the lead in providing capacity-building training for various stakeholders.

(c) Exchange Best Practices

Bangladesh should draw lessons from global best practices in VEO deradicalization and rehabilitation. The case studies of Indonesia and the UK are worth noting here. In Indonesia, the first Anti-Terrorism Law was enacted in 2002 as a presidential directive, later passed in parliament in 2003. The 2003 Anti-Terrorism Law was first amended in 2013 and later in 2018. Three provisions in the Indonesian Anti-Terrorism Law 2018 provide a legal basis for deradicalization and rehabilitation. These include (i) Section 43B (National Preparedness), (ii) Section 43C (Counter-Radicalization), and (iii) Section 43D (Deradicalization).[2] In the United Kingdom, deradicalization and rehabilitation are implemented as part of the Counter-Terrorism Strategy (CONTEST).[3] Prison-based and community-based deradicalization and rehabilitation programs complement the preventive dimensions of CONTEST (Bilzarian 2016; Bologna 2018; UK Home Office 2015).

17.5 Methods of Operation

There are two stages in the risks and needs assessment methods of operation:

(a) Multi-stakeholder consultation

A multi-stakeholder committee is formed to draft a policy directive. The draft shall be aligned with the various interventions discussed in this Handbook. This includes different activities, from risks and needs assessment to multiple forms of counseling and support. The draft shall go through several rounds of stakeholder consultation before the Cabinet approves it. Once the draft receives approval from the Cabinet (Council of Ministers), a Gazette Notification can be issued. This is the shortest possible route for initiating policy reform. This policy directive shall form the basis for further legal reforms to the Anti-Terrorism Act.

(b) Mainstreaming C/PVE Legal and Policy Training

C/PVE legal and policy training shall be mainstreamed in the national curricula so that people develop a fair degree of knowledge and a culture of empathy. Basic and advanced training for law enforcement and intelligence agencies should include national and international best practices.

---

[2] Interview with senior officials of Indonesian National Counter Terrorism Authority (BNPT), December 2022; Institute for Criminal Justice Reform, Indonesia Criminal Law Update (ICLU), Issue No. 3/2018. http://icjr.or.id/wp-content/uploads/2018/11/ICLU-3-2018.pdf.

[3] Claire Brader, "Extremism in Prisons: Are UK Deradicalisation Programmes Working?" 11 June 2020, House of Lords Library. https://lordslibrary.parliament.uk/extremism-in-prisons-are-uk-deradicalisation-programmes-working/.

17.6 Risks and Opportunities/Mitigation Strategies

- **Risks**

Legal and policy reform tend to be very time-consuming. The policy approval process may need to be completed due to a lack of inter-agency coordination or bureaucratic turf battles.

- **Opportunities**

At least three opportunities exist to mitigate the risks of bureaucratic turf battles and facilitate legal and policy reforms. First, there is the highest political will to expand soft approaches to C/PVE. This was evident in the policy statements of Prime Minister Sheikh Hasina, who directed law enforcement agencies to take measures to prevent violent extremism through deradicalization, rehabilitation, and reintegration. Second, there is a consensus among senior MOHA officials on the need for policy and legal reforms for VEO rehabilitation. Third, after implementing several ad hoc initiatives to rehabilitate VEOs, CT agencies have recognized the urgency of getting the legal and policy footing for a wide range of deradicalization and rehabilitation programs.

17.7 Monitoring and Evaluation Framework

(a) Lead Ministry

Bangladesh's lead Ministry for C/PVE is the Ministry of Home Affairs. Senior officials jointly monitor legal reforms for VEO deradicalization and rehabilitation at the MOHA's Public Security and Security Services divisions.

(b) Lead Agency

Bangladesh Police (HQ, ATU, and CTTC) will work closely with the Prison HQ to initiate legal and policy reforms.

(c) Indicator

Two indicators will be used to monitor and evaluate the screening and admission process:

- Indicator 1 (proposal): The number of provisions in the proposed draft legal and policy guidelines.
- Indicator 2 (approval): Number of provisions in the draft legal and policy guidelines approved.

(d) Impact Assessment

Independent researchers should be engaged in conducting an impact assessment of the legal and policy provisions for VEO deradicalization and rehabilitation.

Independent evaluators shall conduct periodic reviews of the legal and policy guidelines.

17.8 Conclusion

In conclusion, legal and policy reforms will clarify the tasks of various VEO rehabilitation practitioners. Senior policymakers and CT agencies agree that such reforms are needed. It is high time such thoughts for reforms were translated into concrete actions.

References

Bilazarian, Talene. 2016. *Countering Violent Extremism: Lessons on Early Intervention from the United Kingdom's Channel Program.* London: GW Program on Extremism.

Bologna, Chiara. 2018. *UNICRI Initiatives: Rehabilitation and Reintegration of Violent Extremist Offenders and Community-Based Projects.* 167th United Nations Asia and Far East Institute for the Prevention of Crime and the Treatment of Offenders (UNAFEI) International Training Course Visiting Experts' Papers. Resource Material Series No. 104. Tokyo: UNAFEI.

UK Home Office. 2015. *Channel Duty Guidance: Protecting vulnerable people from being drawn into terrorism.* London: Home Office.

White House. 2018. *"National Strategy for Counterterrorism of the United States of America"* https://trumpwhitehouse.archives.gov/wp-content/uploads/2018/10/NSCT.pdf.

Zhou, Zunyou. 2019. "Chinese strategy for de-radicalization." *Terrorism and Political Violence* 31 (6): 1187–1209.

Chapter 18
Conclusions: Integration of Efforts

18.1 Introduction

This Handbook has considered deradicalization and rehabilitation useful in countering and preventing violent extremism (C/PVE). It defines deradicalization activities as interventions needed to bring about cognitive and behavioral transformation among VEOs and rehabilitation as strategies for promoting social reintegration. Both are critical for creating a peaceful and resilient society in Bangladesh.

It calls for upholding several core principles of deradicalization and rehabilitation. The list includes:

- Gender sensitivity
- Respect for human rights and the rule of law
- Beneficiaries' safety and security
- Inter-agency coordination
- High-quality intelligence
- Monitoring and evaluation

The Handbook adopts a whole-of-society approach and targets various government, private sector, and civil society stakeholders. It offers both a policy toolkit and a practitioner's guide.

The interventions listed in this Handbook fall into four thematic areas:

- Preparatory stage
- Deradicalization
- Rehabilitation
- Policy Issues

For each stage, this Handbook proposes focused intervention. For each area of intervention, there is a list of critical actors, activities, and methods of operations. The risks that may arise and the opportunities for mitigating the risks are also identified.

I. Ahmed et al., *Handbook on Deradicalization and Rehabilitation of Violent Extremist Offenders in Bangladesh*, SpringerBriefs in Environment, Security, Development and Peace 41, https://doi.org/10.1007/978-3-031-85807-9_18

Each intervention plan concludes with a discussion of the monitoring and evaluation framework.

18.2 Summary of Chapters

This section summarizes various intervention plans laid out in the Handbook.

- *Chapter 2 (Target Beneficiaries):* This chapter provides a comprehensive list of six beneficiary groups: (a) convicted and imprisoned; (b) convicted but released after prison term; (c) under-trial detainees; (d) under-trial on bail; (e) surrendered but not imprisoned; and (f) at-risk communities. It also calls for addressing the deradicalization and rehabilitation needs of all categories of VEOs operating in Bangladesh. They represent three major ideological camps: ethno-nationalist, left-wing, and faith-based Islamist groups.
- *Chapter 3 (Key Actors):* This chapter lists 14 key actors. It argues that law enforcement, intelligence agencies, and prison authorities are key implementing agencies. It emphasizes the role of psychologists, religious counsellors, educational institutions, vocational and skills trainers, and cultural organizations for cognitive and ideological transformation and physical disengagement. Various rehabilitative activities call for the involvement of social workers, business chambers, families of VEOs and victims, civil society, and community gatekeepers. Finally, it suggests the involvement of political actors and the media.
- *Chapter 4 (Capacity Building of Prison Staff and CT Professionals):* This chapter provides a plan for building the capacity of prison staff and CT professionals to implement and coordinate various activities designed for the deradicalization and rehabilitation of VEOs.
- *Chapter 5 (Screening and Admission for Assessing Readiness):* This chapter presents the Militant Activity Risks and Needs Assessment (MARNA) as a basis for determining the readiness of target beneficiaries for deradicalization and rehabilitation. The MARNA tool has four components: risk assessment indicators, assessment scores, qualitative assessment, overall assessment, and intervention plan. It calls for a multi-stakeholder intervention involving security and intelligence agencies, forensic psychologists, and religious counsellors.
- *Chapter 6 (Religious Counselling):* As Islamist militancy has emerged as a significant security threat, this chapter calls for the engagement of religious scholars as a path toward the physical disengagement of VEOs. Among the various activities, it calls for developing a religious counseling module, a religious rehabilitation group, a mobile application, and modernizing Imam training.
- *Chapter 7 (Psychological Intervention):* This chapter provides a list of activities to be carried out to disengage an individual from extremist ideas for cognitive behavioral transformation.

- *Chapter 8 (Cultural Orientation):* This chapter highlights the role of cultural and sporting activities in creating a healthy society. Cultural orientation will be given by promoting Bangladeshi culture, heritage, and language and engaging the youth in various sporting competitions.
- *Chapter 9 (Social Harmony, Pluralism, and Tolerance through Education):* This chapter argues that tolerance education can be crucial in countering intolerance and violent extremism by promoting social harmony, pluralism, and tolerance. By providing the VEOs with a comprehensive and nuanced understanding of different cultures, religions, and perspectives, education can help them develop empathy and respect for others.
- *Chapter 10 (Legal Counselling):* This chapter lays out a plan for CT professionals and legal aid service providers in Bangladesh to disseminate the knowledge of the Anti Terrorism Act and other relevant laws and policies as an instrument for C/PVE. It is assumed that knowledge of the emerging body of laws will prevent an individual from holding extremist ideas or planning to conduct a terrorist attack.
- *Chapter 11 (Physical Disengagement):* This chapter discusses how an individual, whether a convict in prison, an under-trial suspect on bail, or a person vulnerable to recruitment and radicalization, can be physically disengaged from a terrorist activity or group. The roles of the prison authorities, CT agencies, families, and other social actors are emphasized in motivating, training, and monitoring an individual.
- *Chapter 12 (Academic Training):* This chapter stresses the need to extend educational opportunities for various beneficiaries, such as those who could not finish their studies or wish to continue after an interval. It argues that education and skills will enhance critical thinking ability and enable a person to pursue a meaningful livelihood opportunity.
- *Chapter 13 (Vocational Skills Training):* This chapter provides a plan for promoting technical and vocational education and training (TVET) as an instrument for deradicalization and rehabilitation.
- *Chapter 14 (Employment and Entrepreneurial Support):* This chapter discusses the need for extending employment opportunities and entrepreneurial support to rehabilitate VEOs. The roles of CT agencies, business chambers, financial institutions, and prison authorities are highlighted. A need assessment tool is annexed to match the demand and supply sides.
- *Chapter 15 (Support for the Family and Community Members):* VEOs' families and community members will be essential in implementing a deradicalization and rehabilitation strategy. Hence, this chapter discusses how CT agencies, counsellors, and educational institutions can provide various support services to VEOs' families and communities.
- *Chapter 16 (Resettlement Support):* This chapter proposes a multi-stakeholder plan for resetting a post-release convicted VEO. Physical resettlement, social reintegration, and surveillance are expected to be vital in implementing this plan.
- *Chapter 17 (Policy Reforms):* This chapter stresses the need for a designed legal and policy framework for the deradicalization and rehabilitation of VEOs. The Ministry of Home Affairs (MoHA), in collaboration with other ministries of the

Government of Bangladesh, will initiate the reforms. Some reforms are underway, such as the Bangladesh Police adopting the *CTTC Strategy for Countering Violent Extremism in Bangladesh.*

18.3 Integration of Efforts

The term 'integration of efforts' refers to the fusion of various activities by multiple ministries and actors. This section provides a four-pronged strategy for coordination and cooperation among multiple actors, ministries, and national committees in implementing the Handbook for VEO deradicalization and rehabilitation.

(a) Role of National Coordination Bodies

The National Committee for Security Affairs (NCSA), the National Committee for Intelligence Coordination (NCIC), and the National Committee for Militancy Resistance and Prevention (NCMRP) are three apex coordinating bodies having mandates in the domain of C/PVE. These coordination bodies will provide national guidelines to coordinate and synthesize all counterterrorism-related activities in Bangladesh. The NCSA will provide a national security perspective, the NCIC will emphasize intelligence fusion, and the NCMRP will focus on inter-ministerial coordination. Among the intelligence agencies, the Directorate General of Forces Intelligence (DGFI), the National Security Intelligence (NSI), and the Special Branch (SB)have a role to play in risk assessment, surveillance, and monitoring of VEOs. The NCIC will issue timely directives to coordinate the activities of DGFI, NSI, and SB.

(b) Inter-Ministerial Coordination

As discussed throughout this Handbook, implementing a strategy for the deradicalization and rehabilitation of VEOs will involve various GoB ministries. MoHA will take the lead but must coordinate its efforts with other line ministries. The list includes the Ministry of Agriculture, Ministry of Commerce, Ministry of Cultural Affairs, Ministry of Education, Ministry of Labour and Employment, Ministry of Religious Affairs, Ministry of Youth and Sports, and Ministry of Women and Children Affairs.

(c) Coordination among Actors

A Deradicalization Intervention and Rehabilitation Coordination Team (DIRECT) will be formed to facilitate coordination among various actors. The Police HQ may lead the DIRECT with delegates from the Anti Terrorism Unit (ATU), Counter Terrorism and Transnational Crime (CTTC), Rapid Action Battalion (RAB), and the Prisons Directorate. DIRECT will form thematic working groups for psychological counseling, religious counseling, education and skills training, and civil society engagement. Various private and civil sector actors will join the working groups.

(d) Knowledge Sharing

A virtual Knowledge Hub will be developed to share best practices in VEO deradicalization and rehabilitation. The Hub will showcase existing national and international best practices and share the findings of the independent impact assessment.

18.4 Future Directions

This Handbook is the first in South Asia to mainstream deradicalization and rehabilitation in the C/PVE strategy. There is a strong political will among senior government officials and CT agencies to adopt the Handbook as a basis for guiding intervention plans by various actors. The prison authorities and other actors have also shown tremendous support for adopting such a Handbook. Transforming such commitment and enthusiasm into a sustained action is now a call of time. As Bangladesh embarks on implementing a structured plan for the deradicalization and rehabilitation of VEOs, it will need to continuously upgrade the Handbook in light of lessons learned, independent evaluation, and international best practices.

On the Authors

Dr. Imtiaz Ahmed is the Executive Director of the Centre for Alternatives, Bangladesh, and a retired Professor of International Relations at the University of Dhaka. He is also an Adjunct Professor at Taylor's University, Malaysia. He has authored, co-authored, and edited 57 books and 22 monographs, published 129 research papers in leading national and international journals, and edited volumes. His recent publications are the following books: *Rights, Rivers, and the Quest for Water Commons: The Case of Bangladesh* (Berlin, 2021); *Rohingyas in Myanmar and Bangladesh: The Violence-Protection Dialectic and the Narratives of Certain Unsafety/Uncertain Safety*, co-authored with Niloy Ranjan Biswas (Dhaka and London, 2022); *Imagining Post-Covid Education Futures*, edited (Dhaka, 2023); *Celebrating 100 Years of the University of Dhaka: Reflections from Alumni—National and International,* in 7 Volumes, edited (Dhaka, 2023). His latest edited book is *The Changing Nature of Geopolitics and the Futures of Bangladesh* (Dhaka, 2022-2024). Email: imtiazalter@gmail.com.

I. Ahmed et al., *Handbook on Deradicalization and Rehabilitation of Violent Extremist Offenders in Bangladesh*, SpringerBriefs in Environment, Security, Development and Peace 41, https://doi.org/10.1007/978-3-031-85807-9

ASM Ali Ashraf is a Professor and Chair of the Department of International Relations at the University of Dhaka. He holds a Ph.D. in International Security Policy from the University of Pittsburgh. He specializes in international security, counterterrorism, migration, and public policy. He is a regular speaker at the Defence Services Command and Staff College, Foreign Service Academy, National Defence College, and Police Staff College in Bangladesh. He received the J. William Fulbright and the European Union Center of Excellence Dissertation Fellowship. His edited and co-edited books include *Intelligence, National Security, and Foreign Policy: A South Asian Narrative* (BILIA, 2016), *The Futures of Borders and Geopolitics in South Asia: Beyond a Statist Discourse* (Palgrave, 2024), and *Intelligence Services in South Asia: Colonial Past and Post-Colonial Realities* (Routledge, 2025). *Email:* aliashraf@du.ac.bd.

Niloy Ranjan Biswas is a Professor in the Department of International Relations, University of Dhaka, Dhaka-1000, Bangladesh. Email: niloy@du.ac.bd.

Dr. Niloy Ranjan Biswas is a Professor at the Department of International Relations, University of Dhaka. In 2016, he completed his Ph.D. in International Politics at the City University of London. In 2017, he completed the United States Institute of Peace (USIP)-Resolve Fellowship to conduct a post-doctoral study on community policing and its challenges in preventing violent extremism. Dr. Biswas has several academic and policy publications to his credit. He has co-authored with Professor Imtiaz Ahmed his first book on *Rohingyas in Myanmar and Bangladesh: The Violence-Protection Dialectic and the Narratives of Certain Unsafety/Uncertain Safety*, published by the University of Dhaka and University College London; co-edited five books and authored forty journal articles and book chapters. He has written extensively on law-enforcement agencies, deradicalization and preventing violent extremism, refugees and forced migration, security governance reform, and United Nations peace support endeavors. *Email:* niloy@du.ac.bd.

The manufacturer's authorised representative in the EU is Springer Nature Customer Service Centre GmbH, Europaplatz 3, 69115 Heidelberg, Germany. If you have any concerns regarding our products, please contact ProductSafety@springernature.com

Printed and bound by CPI Group (UK) Ltd, Croydon, CR0 4YY
30/09/2026
02225575-0016